THE ATTACK
AND OTHER PAPERS

R. H. TAWNEY

The Attack

and
Other Papers

with a foreword by
Tony Benn MP

SPOKESMAN

First published in 1953 by George Allen & Unwin Ltd.

This edition published in 1981 by Spokesman, Bertrand Russell House, Gamble Street, Nottingham NG7 4ET.

British Library Cataloguing in Publication Data

Tawney, R.H.
The attack.
1. England — Historiography
I. Title
907' .2042 DA1
ISBN 0 85124 312 6

Printed by the Russell Press Ltd, Nottingham.

To
Richard Rees

"*Forsooth, brethren, fellowship is heaven, and lack of fellowship is hell: fellowship is life, and lack of fellowship is death: and the deeds that ye do upon the earth, it is for fellowship's sake that ye do them, and the life that is in it, that shall live on and on for ever, and each one of you part of it, while many a man's life upon the earth from the earth shall wane. Therefore I bid you not dwell in hell but in heaven, or while ye must, upon earth, which is a part of heaven, and forsooth no foul part.*"

William Morris A DREAM OF JOHN BALL

PREFACE

THE papers contained in this volume were published, with two exceptions, between the beginning of the first World War and the end of the second. The majority of them are printed, apart from minor changes, in the form in which they first appeared. When more substantial alterations have been made a statement to that effect has been included in a foot-note. It did not seem right either to repeat opinions made untenable by events or, by a silent substitution of others for them, to affect a prescience which the author did not possess.

My thanks are due to the British Academy, Messrs. Routledge and Kegan Paul, *The Times Educational Supplement*, The *Manchester Guardian*, the *New Statesman and Nation*, and the *Political Quarterly* for permission to reprint work first published by them. My debt to my wife and to the friend to whom this book is dedicated is beyond acknowledgment.

R. H. T.

Foreword to 1981 Edition

Political argument in Britain today is becoming more fundamental as the old consensus breaks down under the inherent defects of capitalism. This breakdown is, in turn, dissolving the modest welfare society which had been established and eroding liberalism itself.

Never has democratic socialism been more necessary, but never has its struggle to assert itself been more difficult. First, because it is constantly and maliciously misrepresented by a mass media which increasingly acts as a propaganda machine rather than an information service. And, secondly, because it suffers from the experience of Labourism under successive Labour Governments since the second World War, which often was not socialism even though it was presented as such both by its advocates and its opponents.

The price we have paid for failing to establish even a base for socialism over the last thirty years is that a renewed and most virulent strain of capitalism is now in the ascendancy.

The only 'opposition' being permitted to be heard by the establishment is a weak centralist liberalism which can, on occasion, misappropriate the word 'socialism' behind which authoritarian forces can muster and the trade union movement can be broken.

Resistance to monetarism or the imposition of the old consensus wrapped in new coalition alignments cannot be entrusted to an opposition rhetoric which simply heaps abuse upon ministers carrying out traditional capitalist remedies. The true nature of this crisis must be understood and explained. This understanding and this explanation must be widely spread before socialist answers can be evolved as a guide for the future. It is at this very moment that the Labour Party is coming to realise the price it has paid for its long neglect of socialism, as a tool of analysis; as a set of moral values; and as the inspiration for both political action and political education.

Fortunately, the Labour movement has its own tradition of socialist writing upon which it can call, and none greater than came from R.H. Tawney. The papers which he wrote, now reprinted in this book, are a part of that inheritance, and will give a new generation of socialists an insight into the unique nature of Tawney's mind, morality and motivation.

His analysis will greatly encourage those in the movement who are now seeking to rediscover the socialist critique of capitalism and re-establish the socialist response to what is happening.

For some years Tawney has been quoted extensively by the right-wing of the Labour Party who have seemed to appropriate him as the Father of their own school of thought. The Social Democrats, whether they have left the Party to fight against socialism from the outside, or whether they have stayed to fight socialism from within the Party, have both laid claim to be Tawney's true disciples, and then to use his name to represent the socialist majority in the Party as being a new breed of socialists who are outside the democratic tradition.

Yet, as the readers of this book will quickly learn, Tawney identified many of the key political issues upon which socialists are now focusing; and he charted, well ahead of his time, the course which they are following. In the remarkable chapter "The choice before the Labour Party" he referred to the 1929-31 MacDonald Government in these terms:

> "The degeneration of socialist parties on assuming office is now an old story . . . what was tried and found wanting was, in short, not merely two years of a Labour Cabinet but a decade of Labour politics."

And again:

> "The gravest weakness of British Labour is its lack of creed. The

Labour Party is hesitant in action because divided in mind. It does not achieve what it could because it does not know what it wants."

Tawney was clear about the meaning of a political creed. He saw it as "a common conception of the ends of political action, and of the means of achieving them, based on a common view of the life proper to human beings, and of the steps required at any moment more nearly to attain it".

Then, his argument established, Tawney spells out his socialist objectives with great simplicity:

"The fundamental question, as always, is: Who is to be master? Is the reality behind the decorous drapery of political democracy to continue to be the economic power wielded by a few thousand — or, if that be preferred, a few hundred thousand — bankers, industrialists, and landowners? Or shall a serious effort be made — as serious, for example, as was made, for other purposes, during the war — to create organs through which the nation can control, in co-operation with other nations, its economic destinies; plan its business as it deems most conducive to the general well-being; override, for the sake of economic efficiency, the obstruction of vested interests; and distribute the product of its labours in accordance with some generally recognised principles of justice? Capitalist parties presumably accept the first alternative. A Socialist Party chooses the second. The nature of its business is determined by its choice."

Today, this statement has acquired a renewed significance, though in the light of our experience of state authorities in various forms, the democratic left would want to emphasise self-management and the decentralisation of initiative and control to protect us from the abuses of central power.

Tawney accepted the "existence of a class struggle" and argued for the "transference of economic power to public hands" which in his view had to "take precedence over the mere alleviation of distress".

Thus, he placed himself firmly on the side of all those within the Labour Party who are now calling for socialism in place of the weak and woolly liberalism which so deeply penetrated Labour politics during the last thirty years.

One of the most scurrilous charges levelled by the right-wing against socialists in the Labour Party is that our policies would endanger political liberty. Tawney meets that charge head on and rebuts it completely.

> ". . . the suggestion that capitalism, at the present stage of its history is the guardian of any liberties but its own is an implausible affectation . . . it would more properly be described as the parent of a new feudalism."

He sees a serious danger that if the conditions of freedom are too long delayed "the failure to achieve it may discredit democracy". He argued that the next Labour Government should "make its central objective to bring the key points of the economic system under public control; should have its measures for attacking that objective prepared in advance; . . . should introduce them at once, in the first months of taking office, while its prestige is still high; and should stand to its guns to the point, if necessary, of a dissolution".

Later in the book, Tawney places all this argument in its proper moral framework. As a convinced democrat and Christian socialist he saw Marx as being "as saturated with ethics as a Hebrew prophet" and argues that "Christianity and popular communism — though not it appears the official variety — are alike in holding the now unfashionable view that principles really matter". Tawney constantly reaffirms his commitment to socialism by consent:

> "It is not certain, though it is probable, that socialism can, in England, be achieved by the methods proper to democracy. It is certain that it cannot be achieved by any other; nor even if it could should the supreme goods of civil and political liberty in whose absence no socialism worthy of the name can breathe, be part of the price."

And these arguments have a direct relevance to our debates today. There is nothing in this book to support the Social Democrats or the right of the Labour Party in their continuing attacks upon democratic socialism. This book is, indeed, a textbook for the democratic left which is now steadily —

and rightly — expanding its influence within the whole movement.

And nothing would have given Tawney more satisfaction since he was a teacher, not a candidate for office, and he saw socialism coming up from the bottom, born out of experience, tested in struggle, inspired by moral values and its policies subjected to the rigid test of analysis and implemented by democratic means. It is, in my judgement, highly significant that Tawney should have arrived at his conclusions after a lifetime in the Adult Education movement. He clearly learned as much from his students as he taught them. His own teaching was obviously enriched by what had happened to them; and he saw clearly that the socialism he believed in could only be brought about if it was understood to be relevant to the lives of working people. Similarly he deeply believed that democracy itself depended for its survival and growth upon a clear commitment to it by those who needed democracy and who had to make it work.

At a moment in history when socialism is under attack and when our democratic liberties are being eroded Tawney's teachings have a special relevance to the Party, the movement and the world.

Tony Benn

eye, the bewildering tumult seemed to grow more insistent with the growing brilliance of the atmosphere and the intenser blue of the July sky. The sound was different, not only in magnitude, but in quality, from anything known to me. It was not a succession of explosions or a continuous roar; I, at least, never heard either a gun or a bursting shell. It was not a noise; it was a symphony. It did not move; it hung over us. It was as though the air were full of a vast and agonised passion, bursting now into groans and sighs, now into shrill screams and pitiful whimpers, shuddering beneath terrible blows, torn by un-earthly whips, vibrating with the solemn pulse of enormous wings. And the supernatural tumult did not pass in this direction or that. It did not begin, intensify, decline, and end. It was poised in the air, a stationary panorama of sound, a condition of the atmosphere, not the creation of man. It seemed that one had only to lift one's eyes to be appalled by the writhing of the tormented element above one, that a hand raised ever so little above the level of the trench would be sucked away into a whirlpool revolving with cruel and incredible velocity over infinite depths. And this feeling, while it filled one with awe, filled one also with triumphant exultation, the exultation of struggling against a storm in mountains, or watching the irresistible course of a swift and destructive river. Yet at the same time one was intent on practical details, wiping the trench dirt off the bolt of one's rifle, reminding the men of what each was to do, and when the message went round, "five minutes to go," seeing that all bayonets were fixed. My captain, a brave man and a good officer, came along and borrowed a spare watch off me. It was the last time I saw him. At 7.30 we went up the ladders, doubled through the gaps in the wire, and lay down, waiting for the line to form up on each side of us. When it was ready we went forward, not doubling, but at a walk. For we had nine hundred yards of rough ground to the trench which was our first objective, and about fifteen hundred to a further trench where we were to wait for orders. There was a bright light in the air, and the tufts of coarse grass were grey with dew.

I hadn't gone ten yards before I felt a load fall from me. There's a sentence at the end of *The Pilgrim's Progress* which has always struck me as one of the most awful things imagined

by man: "Then I saw that there was a way to Hell, even
from the Gates of Heaven, as well as from the City of Destruction." To have gone so far and be rejected at last! Yet
undoubtedly man walks between precipices, and no one knows
the rottenness in him till he cracks, and then it's too late. I had
been worried by the thought: "Suppose one should lose one's
head and get other men cut up! Suppose one's legs should take
fright and refuse to move!" Now I knew it was all right.
I shouldn't be frightened and I shouldn't lose my head.
Imagine the joy of that discovery! I felt quite happy and
self-possessed. It wasn't courage. That, I imagine, is the
quality of facing danger which one knows to be danger, of
making one's spirit triumph over the bestial desire to live in
this body. But I knew that I was in no danger. I knew I shouldn't
be hurt; knew it positively, much more positively than I know
most things I'm paid for knowing. I understood in a small way
what Saint-Just meant when he told the soldiers who protested
at his rashness that no bullet could touch the emissary of the
Republic. And all the time, in spite of one's inner happiness,
one was shouting the sort of thing that N.C.O.s do shout and
no one attends to: "Keep your extension"; "Don't bunch";
"Keep up on the left." I remember being cursed by an orderly
for yelling the same things days after in a field-hospital.

Well, we crossed three lines that had once been trenches,
and tumbled into the fourth, our first objective. "If it's all like
this it's a cake-walk," said a little man beside me, the kindest
and bravest of friends, whom no weariness could discourage
or danger daunt, a brick-layer by trade, but one who could
turn his hand to anything, the man whom of all others I would
choose to have beside me at a pinch; but he's dead. While
the men dug furiously to make a fire-step, I looked about me.
On the parados lay a wounded man of another battalion, shot,
to judge by the blood on his tunic, through the loins or stomach.
I went to him, and he grunted, as if to say, "I am in terrible
pain; you must do something for me; you must do something
for me." I hate touching wounded men—moral cowardice, I
suppose. One hurts them so much and there's so little to be
done. I tried, without much success, to ease his equipment,
and then thought of getting him into the trench. But it was
crowded with men and there was no place to put him. So I left

him. He grunted again angrily, and looked at me with hatred as well as pain in his eyes. It was horrible. It was as though he cursed me for being alive and strong when he was in torture. I tried to forget him by snatching a spade from one of the men and working fiercely on the parapet. But one's mind wasn't in it; it was over "there," there where "they" were waiting for us. Far away, a thousand yards or so half-left, we could see tiny kilted figures running and leaping in front of a dazzlingly white Stonehenge, manikins moving jerkily on a bright green cloth. "The Jocks bombing them out of Mametz," said someone, whether rightly or not, I don't know. Then there was a sudden silence, and when I looked round I saw the men staring stupidly, like calves smelling blood, at two figures. One was doubled up over his stomach, hugging himself and frowning. The other was holding his hand out and looking at it with a puzzled expression. It was covered with blood—the fingers, I fancy, were blown off—and he seemed to be saying: "Well, this is a funny kind of thing to have for a hand." Both belonged to my platoon; but our orders not to be held up attending to the wounded were strict. So, I'm thankful to say, there was no question what to do for them. It was time to make for our next objective, and we scrambled out of the trench.

I said it was time for us to advance again. In fact, it was, perhaps, a little more. By my watch we were three minutes over-due, not altogether a trifle. The artillery were to lift from the next trench at the hour fixed for us to go forward. Our delay meant that the Germans had a chance of reoccupying it, supposing them to have gone to earth under the bombardment. Anyway, when we'd topped a little fold in the ground, we walked straight into a zone of machine-gun fire. The whole line dropped like one man, some dead and wounded, the rest taking instinctively to such cover as the ground offered. On my immediate right three men lay in a shell-hole. With their heads and feet just showing, they looked like fish in a basket.

In crossing no-man's-land we must have lost many more men than I realised then. For the moment the sight of the Germans drove everything else out of my head. Most men, I suppose, have a palaeolithic savage somewhere in them, a beast that occasionally shouts to be given a chance of showing his joyful cunning in destruction. I have, anyway, and from

the age of catapults to that of shot-guns always enjoyed aiming
at anything that moved, though since manhood the pleasure
has been sneaking and shamefaced. Now it was a duty to
shoot, and there was an easy target. For the Germans were
brave men, as brave as lions. Some of them actually knelt
—one for a moment even stood—on the top of their parapet,
to shoot, within not much more than a hundred yards of us. It
was insane. It seemed one couldn't miss them. Every man
I fired at dropped, except one. Him, the boldest of the lot, I
missed more than once. I was puzzled and angry. Three hundred years ago I should have tried a silver bullet. Not that I
wanted to hurt him or anyone else. It was missing I hated.
That's the beastliest thing in war, the damnable frivolity. One's
like a merry, mischievous ape tearing up the image of God.
When I read now the babble of journalists about "the sporting
spirit of our soldiers," it makes me almost sick. God forgive us
all! But then it was as I say.

When the remaining Germans got back into their trench I
stopped firing and looked about me. Just in front of me lay a
boy who had been my batman till I sacked him for slackness.
I had cursed him the day before for being drunk. He lay
quite flat, and might have been resting, except for a big ragged
hole at the base of his skull where a bullet had come out. His
closest friend, also a bit of a scallywag, was dead beside him.
Next to me a man was trying with grimy hands to dab a field-
dressing on to the back of a lance-corporal, shot, it seemed,
through the chest, who was clutching his knees and rocking to
and fro. He was one of two much-respected brothers, of whom
the other had been badly wounded beside me some months
before, partly, I fear, through imprudence on my part in taking
him to explore a sap where we had no business in daytime to
be. My platoon officer lay on his back. His face and hands
were as white as marble. His lungs were labouring like a
bellows worked by machinery. But his soul was gone. He
was really dead already; in a minute or two he was what the
doctors call "dead." "Is there any chance for us, sergeant?"
a man whispered. I said it would be all right; the ——'s
would be coming through us in an hour, and we would go
forward with them. All the same, it looked as if they wouldn't
find much except corpses.

The worst of it was the confusion; one didn't know how many of us were living or where they were. I crawled along the line to see. A good many men were lying as they'd dropped, where they couldn't have hit anything but each other. Those able to move crawled up at once when spoken to, all except one, who buried his head in the ground and didn't move. I think he was crying. I told him I'd shoot him, and he came up like a lamb. Poor boy, he could have run from there to our billets before I'd have hurt him. I wriggled back, and told the only officer left that I'd seen some twenty men or so fit for something, and our right flank in the air. Then I realised that, like a fool, I'd forgotten to find out who, if anyone, from other units was beyond us on our right, one of the very things which I'd crawled down the line to see. So I told a man near me to take an order to establish contact, if there was anyone with whom to make it. Like a brave fellow he at once left the comparative safety of his shell-hole; but I'd hardly turned my head when a man said, "He's hit." That hurt me. It was as if I'd condemned him to death. Anyway, I'd see to the left flank, where our "A" Company should have been, myself.

The officer, a boy, was—no blame to him—at the end of his tether. He protested, but in the end let me go. If "A" Company had made a muddle and stuck half-way, it seemed a bright idea to get them into line with what was left of us. In five minutes, I thought, I shall be back, and with any luck we shall have part of another company on our left, and perhaps be able to rush the trench. Of course it was idiotic. If our company had lost half or more of its strength, why should "A" Company have fared any better? But, there! I suppose the idea of death in the mass takes a lot of hammering into one before one grasps it. Anyway, as I crawled back, first straight back, and then off to my right, everything seemed peaceful enough. One couldn't believe that the air a foot or two above one's head was deadly. The weather was so fine and bright that the thought of death, if it had occurred to me, which it didn't, would have seemed absurd. Then I saw a knot of men lying down away to the right. I didn't realise that they were dead or wounded, and waved to them, "Reinforce." When they didn't move, I knelt up and waved again.

I don't know what most men feel like when they're wounded.

What I felt was that I had been hit by a tremendous iron
hammer, swung by a giant of inconceivable strength, and then
twisted with a sickening sort of wrench so that my head and
back banged on the ground, and my feet struggled as though
they didn't belong to me. For a second or two my breath
wouldn't come. I thought—if that's the right word—"This is
death," and hoped it wouldn't take long. By-and-by, as nothing
happened, it seemed I couldn't be dying. When I felt the
ground beside me, my fingers closed on the nose-cap of a shell.
It was still hot, and I thought absurdly, in a muddled way,
This is what has got me." I tried to turn on my side, but the
pain, when I moved, was like a knife, and stopped me dead.
There was nothing to do but lie on my back. After a few
minutes two men in my platoon crawled back past me at a few
yards' distance. They saw me and seemed to be laughing,
though of course they weren't, but they didn't stop. Probably
they were wounded. I could have cried at their being so cruel.
It's being cut off from human beings that's as bad as anything
when one's copped it badly, and, when a lad wriggled up to me
and asked, "What's up, sergeant?" I loved him. I said, "Not
dying, I think, but pretty bad," and he wriggled on. What else
could he do?

I raised my knees to ease the pain in my stomach, and at
once bullets came over; so I put them down. Not that I much
minded dying now or thought about it. By a merciful arrangement, when one's half-dead the extra plunge doesn't seem very
terrible. One's lost part of one's interest in life. The roots are
loosened, and seem ready to come away without any very
agonising wrench. Tolstoi's account of the death of Prince
Andrew is true, though I can't imagine how he knew unless
he'd been to the edge of things himself. Anyway, though the
rational part of me told me to lie flat, my stomach insisted
on my knees going up again, in spite of the snipers, and it didn't
bother me much when they began shelling the trench about
sixty to eighty yards behind me, with heavies. One heard them
starting a long way off, and sweeping towards one with a
glorious rush, like the swift rustling of enormous and incredibly
powerful pinions. Then there was a thump, and I was covered
with earth. After about the thirtieth thump something hit me
in the stomach and took my wind. I thought, "Thank heaven,

it's over this time," but it was only an extra heavy sod of earth. So the waiting began again. It was very hot. To save what was left of my water, I tried one of the acid-drops issued the night before, the gift, I suppose, of some amiable lunatic in England. It tasted sweet, and made me feel sick. I drank the rest of my water at a gulp. How I longed for the evening! I'd lost my watch, so I tried to tell the time by the sun, cautiously shifting my tin hat off my eyes to have a peep. It stood straight overhead in an enormous arch of blue. After an age I looked again. It still stood in the same place, as though performing a miracle to plague me. I began to shout feebly for stretcher-bearers, calling out the name of my battalion and division, as though that would bring men running from all points of the compass. Of course it was imbecile and cowardly. They couldn't hear me, and, if they could, they oughtn't to have come. It was asking them to commit suicide. But I'd lost my self-respect. I hoped I should faint, but couldn't.

*   *   *

It was a lovely evening, and a man stood beside me. I caught him by the ankle, in terror lest he should vanish. In answer to his shouts—he was an R.A.M.C. corporal—a doctor came and looked at me. Then, promising to return in a minute, they went off to attend to someone else. That was the worst moment I had. I thought they were deceiving me—that they were leaving me for good. A man badly knocked out feels as though the world had spun him off into a desert of unpeopled space. Combined with pain and helplessness, the sense of abandonment goes near to break his heart. I did so want to be spoken kindly to, and I began to whimper, partly to myself, partly aloud. But they came back, and, directly the doctor spoke to his orderly, I knew he was one of the best men I had ever met. He can't have been more than twenty-six or twenty-seven; but his face seemed to shine with love and comprehension, not of one's body only, but of one's soul, and with the joy of spending freely a wisdom and goodness drawn from inexhaustible sources. He listened like an angel while I told him a confused, non-sensical yarn about being hit in the back by a nose-cap. Then he said I had been shot with a rifle-bullet through the chest and abdomen, put a stiff bandage round me, and gave me morphia. Later, though not then, remembering the change in his voice when he told me what was amiss, I realised that he thought I was done for. Anyway, there was nothing more he could do. No stretcher-bearers were to hand, so it was out of the question to get me in that night. But, after I had felt that divine compassion flow over me, I didn't care. I was like a dog kicked and bullied by everyone that's at last found a kind master, and in a grovelling kind of way I worshipped him. He made his orderly get into a trench when I told him they were sniping, but he wouldn't keep down or go away himself. Perhaps he knew that he couldn't be hit or that it would be well with him if he were.

*   *   *

We attacked, I think, about 820 strong. I've no official figures of casualties. A friend, an officer in "C" Company, which was in support and shelled to pieces before it could start, told me in hospital that we lost 450 men that day, and that, after being put in again a day or two later, we had 54 left. I suppose it's worth it.

Ço dist la Geste e cil ki el' camp fut.

2

Some Reflections of a Soldier[1]

I⊤ is very nice to be at home again. Yet am I at home? One sometimes doubts it. There are occasions when I feel like a visitor among strangers whose intentions are kindly, but whose modes of thought I neither altogether understand nor altogether approve. I find myself storing impressions, attempting hasty and unsatisfactory summaries, to appease the insatiable curiosity of the people with whom I really am at home, the England that's not an island or an empire, but a wet populous dyke stretching from Flanders to the Somme. And then, just when my pencil is on the paper, I realise how hopeless it is. I used to sit at the feet of a philosopher, who thought he had established a common intellectual medium between himself and an Indian friend, till the latter elucidated his position by an hypothesis. "Let us suppose," he said, "that God has chosen to assume the form of an elephant." With the concrete aloofness of that oriental imagery, my teacher strove in vain. The depth of the dividing chasm was revealed by the bridge.

And somewhat the same difficulty troubles me. As we exchange views, one of you assumes as possible or probable something that seems to us preposterous, or dismisses as too trivial for comment what appears to us a fact of primary importance. You speak lightly, you assume that we shall speak lightly, of things, emotions, states of mind, human relationships and affairs, which are to us solemn or terrible. You seem ashamed, as if they were a kind of weakness, of the ideas which

[1] October 1916, published in the *Nation*.

sent us to France, and for which thousands of sons and lovers have died. You calculate the profits to be derived from "War after the War," as though the unspeakable agonies of the Somme were an item in a commercial proposition. You make us feel that the country to which we've returned is not the country for which we went out to fight. And your reticence as to the obvious physical facts of war! And your ignorance as to the sentiments of your relations about it!

Yet I don't think I'm mad, for I find that other soldiers have somewhat the same experience as myself. Not that I profess to speak for the Army! I leave that to the officers who periodically return to Parliament and tell it that the men at the front demand this, or object to that. I say "we," because I find it difficult to separate opinions that I've formed myself from those formed for me by the men with whom I lived, the chance conversations snatched during a slack time in the trenches, or the comments of our mess when the newspapers arrived with Lloyd George's latest rhapsody about "cheerful Tommies with the glint of battle in their eyes," or *The Times* military expert's hundredth variation on the theme that the abstruse science of war consists in killing more of the enemy than he kills of you, so that, whatever its losses—agreeable doctrine—the numerically preponderant side can always win, as it were, by one wicket. We used to blaspheme and laugh and say, "Oh, it's only the papers. People at home can't really be like that." But after some months in England I've come to the conclusion that your journalists don't caricature you so mercilessly as we supposed. No, the fact is we've drifted apart. We have slaved for Rachel, but it looks as if we'd got to live with Leah.

We have drifted apart partly because we have changed and you have not; partly, and that in the most important matters, because we have not changed and you have. Such a cleavage between the civilians who remain civilians and the civilians who become soldiers is, of course, no novelty. It occurred both in the English and the American Civil Wars. It occurred most conspicuously in the French armies of 1793 to 1805 or 1806, in which the Revolution survived as a spell that would charm men to death long after it had become an abomination or a curiosity in Paris. And always it seems to have brought something of the shock of an unexpected discovery to those who,

not having borne the same life of corporate effort and endurance, forget that the unquestioning obedience to which soldiers
are trained is not obedience to popular opinions, and that the
very absence of opportunities for discussion and self-expression
tends, like solitude, to lend weight both to new impressions
and to already formed mental habits. The contrast between
the life which men have left and the unfamiliar duties imposed
upon them creates a ferment, none the less powerful because
often half-unconscious, in all but the least reflective minds. In
particular, when, as has happened in the present war, men
have taken up arms, not as a profession or because forced to
do so by law, but under the influence of some emotion or
principle, they tend to be ruled by the idea which compelled
them to enlist long after it has yielded, among civilians, to
some more fashionable novelty. Less exposed than the civilian
to new intellectual influences, the soldier is apt to retain firmly,
or even to deepen, the impressions which made him, often
reluctantly, a soldier in the first instance. He is like a piece of
stone which, in spite of constant friction, preserves the form
originally struck out in the fires of a volcanic upheaval. How
often, fatigued beyond endurance or horrified by one's actions,
does one not recur to those ideas for support and consolation!
"It is worth it, because——." "It is awful, but I need not
loath myself, because——." We see things which you can only
imagine. We are strengthened by reflections which you have
abandoned. Our minds differ from yours, both because they
are more exposed to change, and because they are less change-
able. While you seem—forgive me if I am rude—to have
been surrendering your creeds with the nervous facility of a
Tudor official, our foreground may be different, but our
background is the same. It is that of August to November,
1914. We are your ghosts.

The contrast reveals itself not less in small things than in
great. It appears as much in the manner in which you visualise
the events of war and interpret to yourselves the duties and
moods of your soldiers as in your conception of the principles
for which we are fighting, and of the kind of harmony, national
and supernational, in which the world may recover stability.
But I am wrong in speaking of "small things and great."
Clearness of vision and sensitiveness of judgment are not

qualities which can be improvised. The ability of men to command them when they need them most is proportionate to the sincerity with which they have habituated themselves to regard matters more accessible and familiar. Therefore I cannot dismiss as trivial the picture which you make to yourselves of war and the mood in which you contemplate that work of art. They are an index of the temper in which you will approach the problems of peace. The war is always beneath your eyes. You read and talk about it, I should say, more constantly than about any other matter. You are anxious to have a truthful account, not of strategy or of other things which are rightly concealed, but of its daily routine and colour, the duties and perplexities, dangers and exposure, toil and occasional repose which make up the life of a soldier at the front. You would wish to enter, as far as human beings can enter, into his internal life, to know how he regards the task imposed upon him, how he conceives his relation to the enemy and to yourselves, from what sources he derives encouragement and comfort. You would wish to know these things; we should wish you to know them. Yet between you and us there hangs a veil. It is mainly of your own unconscious creation. It is not a negative, but a positive, thing. It is not intellectual; it is moral. It is not ignorance (or I should not mention it). It is falsehood. I read your papers and listen to your conversation, and I see clearly that you have chosen to make to yourselves an image of war, not as it is, but of a kind which, being picturesque, flatters your appetite for novelty, for excitement, for easy admiration, without troubling you with masterful emotions. You have chosen, I say, to make an image, because you do not like, or cannot bear, the truth; because you are afraid of what may happen to your souls if you expose them to the inconsistencies and contradictions, the doubts and bewilderment, which lie beneath the surface of things. You are not deceived as to the facts; for facts of this order are not worth official lying. You are deceived as to the Fact. As to that, you may apparently be trusted to lie, *motu proprio et mera voluntate*, to yourselves.

Perhaps this judgment is harsh. Yet when I read the pictures of war given every day in your Press I do not think it is. There are in some of them traits which I recognise as not untrue to life. But the general impression given is tragically false. I can forgive you for representing war as a spectacle, instead of as a state of existence, for I suppose that to the correspondent who is shepherded into an observation post on a show-day it does seem spectacular. But the representation of the human beings concerned is unpardonable. There has been invented a kind of conventional soldier, whose emotions and ideas are those which you find it most easy to assimilate with your coffee and marmalade. And this "Tommy" is a creature at once ridiculous and disgusting. He is represented as invariably "cheerful," as revelling in the "excitement" of war, as finding "sport" in killing other men, as "hunting Germans out of dug-outs as a terrier hunts rats," as overwhelming with kindness the captives of his bow and spear. The last detail is true to life, but the emphasis which you lay upon it is both unintelligent and insulting. Do you expect us to hurt them or starve them? Do you not see that we regard these men who have sat opposite us in mud—"square-headed bastards," as we called them—as the victims of the same catastrophe as ourselves, as our comrades in misery much more truly than you are? Do you think that we are like some of you in accumulating on the head of every wretched antagonist the indignation felt for the wickedness of a government, of a social system, or (if you will) of a nation? For the rest we are depicted as merry assassins, rejoicing in the opportunity of a "scrap" in which we know that more than half our friends will be maimed or killed, careless of our own lives, exulting in the duty of turning human beings into lumps of disfigured clay, light-hearted as children who shoot at sparrows with a new air-gun and clap their hands when they fall, charmed from the transient melancholy of childhood by a game of football or a packet of cigarettes.

Of the first material reality of war, from which everything else takes its colour, the endless and loathsome physical exhaustion, you say little, for it would spoil the piquancy, the verve, of the picture. Of your soldiers' internal life, the constant collision of contradictory moral standards, the liability of the soul to be crushed by mechanical monotony, the difficulty of keeping hold of sources of refreshment, the sensation of taking a profitless part in a game played by monkeys and organised by lunatics, you realise, I think, nothing. Are you

so superficial as to imagine that men do not feel emotions of
which they rarely speak? Or do you suppose that, as a cultured
civilian recently explained to me, these feelings are confined to
"gentlemen," and are not shared by "common soldiers"?
And behind the picture of war given in your papers there
sometimes seems to lurk something worse than, yet allied to,
its untruthfulness, a horrible suggestion that war is somehow,
after all, ennobling; that, if not the proper occupation of man,
it is at least one in which he finds a fullness of self-expression
impossible in peace; that, when clothed in khaki and carrying
rifles, these lads are more truly "men" than they were when
working in offices or factories. Perhaps I do you an injustice.
But that intimation does seem to me to peep through some of
your respectable paragraphs. As I read them, I reflect upon
the friends who, after suffering various degrees of torture, died
in the illusion that war was not the last word of Christian
wisdom. And I have a sensation as of pointed ears and hairy
paws and a hideous ape-face grinning into mine—sin upon sin,
misery upon misery, to the end of the world.

Oh! gentle public—for you were gentle once and may be so
again—put all these delusions from your mind. The reality
is horrible, but it is not so horrible as the grimacing phantom
which you have imagined. Your soldiers are neither so foolish,
nor so brave, nor so wicked, as the mechanical dolls who grin
and kill and grin in the columns of your newspapers. No doubt,
here and there, are boys to whom the holiday from parents
or schoolmasters or employers is an exhilaration, and whose
first impressions—how soon worn out!—are printed by
credulous editors as representing "the spirit of the Army."
Delightful children! To men whose very souls are bleared with
mud, they are as refreshing as spring sunshine after endless
cold and rain. But in the letters of the rank and file who have
spent a winter in the trenches, you will not find war described
as "sport." It is a load that they carry with aching bones,
hating it, and not unconscious of its monstrosity, hoping dimly
that, by shouldering it now, they will save others from it in the
future, looking back with even an exaggerated affection to the
blessings of peace.

They carry their burden with little help from you. For,
when men work in the presence of death, they cannot be

satisfied with conventional justifications of a sacrifice which seems to the poor weakness of our flesh intolerable. They hunger for an assurance which is absolute, for a revelation of the spirit as poignant and unmistakable as the weariness of their suffering bodies. To some of us that revelation has come from France itself, from women who spoke of mercy in the midst of their desolation, or blessed us as they gave us bread. To most of us it must come from you, or not at all. For an army does not live by munitions alone, but also by fellowship in a moral idea or purpose. And that, unless you renew your faith, you cannot give us. You cannot give it us, because you do not possess it. You are, I see, more divided in soul than you were when I became a soldier, denouncing the apostles of war, yet not altogether disinclined to believe that war is an exalting thing, half implying that our cause is the cause of humanity in general and democracy in particular, yet not daring boldly to say so lest later you should be compelled to fulfil your vows, more complacent and self-sufficient in proportion as you are more confident of victory and have less need of other nations, trusting more in the great machine which you have created and less in the unseen forces which, if you will let them, will work on your side. And you are more prone than you were to give way to hatred. Hatred of the enemy is not common, I think, among those who have encountered him. It is incompatible with the proper discharge of our duty. For to kill in hatred is murder; and soldiers, whatever their nationality, are not murderers, but executioners. I know, indeed, how much harder it is for you not to hate than it is for us. You cannot appease the anguish of your losses by feeling, as we feel, that any day your own turn may come. And it is right that there should be a solemn detestation of the sins of Germany, provided that we are not thereby caused to forget our own.

But it is not among those who have suffered most cruelly or whose comprehension of the tragedy is most profound that I find the hatred which appals. For in suffering, as in knowledge, there is something that transcends personal emotion and unites the soul to the suffering and wisdom of God. I find it rather among those who, having no outlet in suffering or in action, seem to discover in hatred the sensation of activity which they have missed elsewhere. They are to be pitied, for they also are seeking a union with their kind, though by a path on which it cannot be found. Nevertheless, the contagion of their spirit is deadly. Every inch that you yield to your baser selves, to hatred, to the materialism which waits on spiritual exhaustion, is added to the deadly space across which the Army must drag itself to its goal and yours. You do not help yourselves, or your country, or your soldiers, by hating, but only by loving and striving to be more lovable. *Pone te ipsum in pace, et tum poteris alios pacificare.*

3

A National College of All Souls[1]

Consider the thousands of brave English people that have been consumed by sea and land within these two years, [who] have not been rogues, cut-purses, horse-stealers, committers of burglary, and other sorts of thieves, as some of our captains and men of war, to excuse themselves, do report. But, in truth, they were young gentlemen, yeomen and yeomen's sons, and artificers of the most brave sort, such as disdained to pilfer and steal, but went as voluntary to serve of a gaiety and joyalty of mind; all which kind of people are the flower and force of a kingdom.

—Sir John Smith to Lord Burghley, January 1589–90.

A LITTLE less than five hundred years ago, a great man desired to commemorate the end of one of the most futile and miserable of wars in which the English nation was ever engaged. He endowed a college "to pray for the souls of all those who fell in the grievous wars between France and England." We stand for a moment where Chichele stood, because we stand upon a world of graves. With a nobler cause we ought not to be content with a memorial less noble. We

[1] February 22, 1917: An amended version of an article published in *The Times Educational Supplement* of that date. Appearing, as it did, when talk of educational reconstruction was in the air, the article was criticised as unduly pessimistic. Unfortunately, it erred on the side of optimism. The emasculation of the Act of 1918 by the post-war "economy" campaign; the equally imposing imbecilities of the subsequent May Report; and the stubborn refusal down to 1939 to implement the recommendations of the Board of Education's Consultative Committee, show that, in referring to the adversaries who, if allowed to work their will, would wreck reform, the author wrote more truly than he knew. The Act of 1944 has since then introduced important improvements which, if allowed a chance, will bear in time abundant fruit. If only one could be certain that the children of darkness will not again be given their heads!

ought to perpetuate in peace the idealism of war, because that alone can deliver us from the selfish appetites that lie in wait for us in both. And, if we desire to perpetuate it, how can we begin better than by founding upon it the educational system to whose influence generation after generation is submitted? It is no time for minimum standards, but for an effort corresponding to the sacrifices which it commemorates. A reconstruction of education in a generous, humane and liberal spirit would be the noblest memorial to those who have fallen, because, though many of them were but little "educated," it would be the most formal and public recognition of the world of the spirit for which they fell. It would show that the nation was prepared to submit its life to principles of the kind for which it thought itself justified in asking them to die.

The fundamental obstacle in the way of education in England is simple. It is that education is a spiritual activity, much of which is not commercially profitable, and that the prevailing temper of Englishmen is to regard as most important that which is commercially profitable, and as of only inferior importance that which is not. The task of those who believe in education is correspondingly simple. It is to induce a larger number of their countrymen to believe, and, if they believe it themselves, to believe more intently, that spiritual activity is of primary importance and worth any sacrifice of material goods, and that, in fostering such activity, education, if not the most powerful, is at least the most readily available agency. Current speech and writing about education often assume that the State is to blame that educational progress is not more rapid, and that, if only it will legislate more swiftly and organise more effectively, the result will be that we shall all be "better educated." And, indeed, legislation and organisation, which should be the mere groundwork and skeleton, are still only too much needed. But, unhappily, the matter is not so simple. To talk as though this or that "reform" were the one thing needed is to deceive ourselves, because, if it had not been for some internal obstacle, some blindness or apathy or recalcitrance within, the reform in question would have been made long ago, or the necessity for it would not have been allowed to arise.

The comparative indifference of English Governments to education—the idea, for example, that the closing of museums, not the closing of expensive restaurants, is the economy most worthy of England, or that any Minister will do for the Board of Education, because no one, thank heaven! is likely to worry *him*, or that the most obvious way of saving money and meeting a shortage of labour is to allow the school life of children to be cut down, because, after all, it does not really very much matter whether the children of mere common wage-earners are educated or not—such indifference is merely a public and faithful interpretation of our attitude towards the things of the spirit, an attitude of sceptical, half-indulgent, half-contemptuous, tolerance. It is the expression of the scale of values which rules in the minds of most individuals, and which, therefore, rules in the State. And we shall not make any serious progress until that scale is reversed, until the English people—and not merely "the State"—is a little horrified at ignorance and vulgarity and stupidity. Courage is a great gift, and deserves to be reverenced. But insight, respect for truth and contempt for charlatanism, a lucid and piercing intelligence which appraises facts for what they are and sees through pompous pretences, are also great gifts. We do not reverence them at all in our ordinary life, and so we cannot command them, even when we would give anything to possess them. We cannot command them, because, as a nation, we value material possessions, and take pains to acquire them, more than we value and take pains to acquire spiritual treasures.

The first step towards educational reform, therefore, is not to start doing more energetically the kind of thing that we used to do in the kind of mood that we used to accept. The first step is to recognise that our mood itself, our attitude towards education, was wrong, and that we shall not be able to change the latter unless we abandon the former, or at least recognise that it ought to be abandoned. The beginning for us, as for all barbarians, is to "burn what we have adored, and to adore what we have burned." True, education may be commended, and just now constantly is commended, on the ground that it is commercially profitable, that it leads to economic success, that it increases national wealth, that it is, in the elegant phrase of the moment, "our principal weapon in the coming commercial war." Those who advocate it for such reasons are, doubtless, correct. But an interest in education which is elicited on these grounds is an insecure foundation for educational reform, because, if it is given for commercial motives, it will also be withdrawn for commercial motives, and because it is the nature of the mind to which such motives are of primary importance to take short views even of commercial profit, and to grudge the disinterested support of the pursuit of knowledge, the postponement of possessing to effort, of enjoyment to toil and thought, without which even material wealth cannot successfully be pursued.

The main need of our day, therefore, is not merely a keener appreciation of the pecuniary possibilities latent, or clamant, in particular kinds of scientific research, but a firmer determination to discard the spiritual crassness, the contempt for disinterested intellectual activity, by which, far more than by deficient commercial acumen, such research, as well as more important things than scientific research, has hitherto been discouraged. And the task of educationalists is not to flatter those who would pick over the treasures of earth and heaven for a piece they can put in their purses—though they may toss them something glittering to play with now and then—but to persuade them that education is to be practised, like other spiritual activities, for itself, "for the glory of God and the relief of man's state," and that, without education, rich men are really poor. Even so their countrymen may not ever believe in education so far as to make sacrifices for it, which is the only test of belief. But then, they do not believe in it now. They will at least come, in time, to respect it. And respect given for right motives is more estimable than patronage and popularity won by appealing to motives which are wrong.

It ought to be easier now than it was three years ago for English people to be persuaded that education is worth any sacrifice. It ought to be easier; because the war has been itself an education. Education is the most formal and public recognition of the claims of the spirit that the modern world has permitted, and the war has thrown certain spiritual tendencies into high relief. It has made moral alternatives intelligible by clothing them with personality. It has caused thousands of people, who are quite without hatred towards Germany, to ask themselves, "What is it in the present German attitude towards life which makes it intolerable to us? Why is it that we feel that

the cause of France and England is the cause of humanity?"
They ask this, and they answer, if they are French or English,
that what is intolerable in the Germany of today, what out-
weighs the many excellences of its learning and public spirit, is
that there is something in it which stamps what it touches with
death, something which is the antithesis of individuality, of
spontaneous personal aspiration and endeavour and sacrifice; a
spirit which organises men but does not inspire them, which
cultivates them but does not love them, which makes a mighty
State, but neither a democracy nor a Church; and that, while
the characteristic sins of France and England, are those of men,
weakness, and passion, and thoughtlessness, the characteristic
sins of Prussia, as she now is, are those of devils, intellectual
arrogance, and a cold heart, and a contempt for what is
lovable and pitiable and ridiculous in human nature.

Soldiers feel this; and, because they feel it, and not merely
because they care about persons like themselves in France or in
England, they not only are willing, but conceive it their duty
to kill and be killed. But both they and we ought to feel more
than this. We ought to recognise that the real struggle, in which
this war is only an episode, is not merely between our own
country and anything so unstable and transitory as modern
Germany, but between permanent and irreconcilable claimants
for the soul of man; and that what makes the German spirit
dangerous is not that it is alien, but that it is horribly congenial,
to almost the whole modern world. For the spirit of German
Imperialism is too often the spirit of English and American
Capitalism, with its cult of power as an end in itself, its
coarse material standards, its subordination of personality to
mechanism, its worship of an elaborate and soul-destroying
organisation; and the materialism, which in Prussia reveals
itself in adoration of the power of the State, in England reveals
itself in adoration of the power of money. The latter is not more
noble, it is more ignoble, because less disinterested, than the
former. If it is not so violent, it is more slyly corrupt, and, as
far as the mass of mankind are concerned, it is almost as
tyrannical. But whether it takes the form of military violence,
or of commercial greed, the spirit of materialism is one, and
the spirit which resists it is one. And if we feel that the absolute
claim of personality, the preservation and development of

spiritual freedom, are worth any sacrifice in time of war, we ought equally to feel that they are worth any sacrifice in time of peace. Now the sphere where the claims of personality are most clearly involved, and where what threatens them is most obviously the operation of materialistic motives, is the sphere of education.

Education offers, indeed, a kind of *experimentum crucis*, an issue on which our sincerity in the causes for which we claim to have taken up arms may be brought to the test. For, ultimately, the merits of a war are judged neither by the diplomatic correspondence which preceded it, nor by the efforts devoted to winning it, but by the kind of civilisation which arises from it, and by the ability of the victor to establish, not only over the enemy, but over himself, the authority of the principles for which he claimed to fight. If, as we claim, the cause of England is the cause of all the higher possibilities of the human spirit, then we ought to perpetuate that cause in our social institutions. The educational system of today was created in the image of our plutocratic, class-conscious selves, and still faithfully reflects them. Worshipping money and social position, we have established for the children of the well-to-do an education lavish even to excess, and have provided for those of four-fifths of the nation the beggarly rudiments thought suitable for helots who would be unserviceable without a minimum of instruction, and undocile helots if spoiled by more. The result has been a system of public education neither venerable, like a college, nor popular, like a public house, but merely indispensable, like a pillar-box. Only those institutions are loved which touch the imagination. Now that the chance has come to make a fresh start, we ought to act on that truth, and think in terms, not of the least that is essential, but of the most that we can achieve. We should provide, not merely, as hitherto, for a small minority, but for all the nation's sons and daughters, an education generous, inspiring, and humane.

4

China, 1930–31[1]

I

OUR host was waiting for us in the restaurant. He had invited some friends to meet us, and the ends of the earth were gathered together. There was a Szechwanese from Chengtu, who had been home once in eighteen years; three men from Kansu, at the other end of China; a Mohammedan, also from Kansu, where Mohammedans sometimes rebel, but who himself, it was explained, was quite civilised and peaceable; and a new arrival from Kokonor, on the borders of Tibet, brown and ruddy like a farmer. He had travelled thirty-seven days, by raft down the Yellow River, by camel, and by train to tell his story to the authorities.

As I nibbled peanuts, and incited the Mohammedan to perform prodigies with the rice-wine by reminding him that alcohol was forbidden by his religion, I caught stray scraps of conversation: "Aeroplanes? No good round us; the mountains are too steep for them to land"; "Taxes paid in advance up to the fortieth year of the Republic"; "The generals in —— make the peasants grow opium so as to tax them higher"; "Yes, but the aborigines won't let us dig for gold." An artisan was crying his wares in a chant under the window. Over all was the sympathetic deference, the radiant courtesy, which is not, as some strangers suppose, a superficial mannerism, but a grace of the spirit.

What is it that makes the unity of China? Not geography, for I should travel to London in less time than it would take

[1] March 1931, published-in the *Manchester Guardian*.

my friend from Szechwan to reach his home in a city that lies a thousand miles from the railway, amid a plain that cunning engineers turned from a desert to a garden by an irrigation scheme planned when Rome was wrestling with Carthage. Not political institutions, for law and government have played a minor part in the past history of China, and, though her present rulers are labouring at the scaffolding, a unitary State is still in its infancy. Not language, for I have an acquaintance who, when she conversed with her sister in the dialect of their home, was told by her mother-in-law to stop talking English. Not community of economic conditions, for, while the south of China is sub-tropical, the north approaches within twelve degrees of the Arctic Circle, and in one district peasants take four crops a year off irrigated land, while in another they maintain a precarious defence against the advance of the desert. Not religion, for in China the gods are not jealous and there is no national creed. Not communications, for there are some 12,000 miles of railway and 35,000 miles of motor-road in a country as large as Europe.

Every fact that a stranger learns tells him that there is not one China, but many. Every day that he passes there he knows more certainly that China is one—one in spite of civil disorder, and military feudalism, and banditry, and extra-territoriality, and foreign settlements and concessions, and the contrast between the twentieth-century economic life of a few cities near the coast and the medieval interior. In no country, not even France, is the impression of a nation, not merely as a political unit or territorial arrangement, but as a human being, so profound and insistent. The personality of the people surrounds a visitor like the tide; while he is peering at one point he is outflanked at another. His reason is still doubting whether China exists as a single organism, and lo! his soul has become half-Chinese.

The cause is less the presence of a generalised type than its absence. It is not that, as in some countries, individuals bear the stamp of a national habit and discipline, but that, in so far as they resemble each other, their resemblance is due to the fact that they are, to an unusual degree, distinct individuals. It is as though personality were everything, and systems nothing. And it is true that political systems have counted for less in

China than elsewhere. The first impulse of most Western observers is to be shocked by her incoherence, and some aspects of it are shocking. They do not always remember, however, the natural facts of which it is the consequence. Hence they unconsciously exaggerate both the disorders of Chinese life and the orderliness of their own. In population, extent of territory, and diversity of conditions, China is to be compared, not with a single European nation, but with Europe as a whole. Problems of political and economic organisation, which in the West are international, are in China domestic; breakdowns, which in the former result in wars between States, in the latter take the form of civil disorder. Her unity, like that of Europe in the Middle Ages, was during the greater part of her history the unity of a civilisation, not of a political system. It rested on the family, which, far more than the State, protected the individual against the effects of economic misfortune and social oppression; on a philosophy which made personal relations, not rules of law, the centre of its scheme; on a sense of the insignificance of the present in the great ocean of the past, which even today causes many Chinese to think in centuries where the West thinks in decades. It was a spirit which was not in haste to put on a body, since it knew that, if it waited, a body would grow round it. Nowhere else does the ticking of time seem so irrelevant to reality.

"Yes, it is distressing. But it is not so bad as at the end of the Han Dynasty, or, for that matter, of the T'ang; or, indeed, now I come to think of it, as on the fall of the Mings." Men rarely in the West console themselves for public misfortunes with the thought that they were worse under the Merovingians and during the Thirty Years War, and the reflection of a Chinese scholar upon present discontents shows the difference of perspective. Things elsewhere forgotten are in China remembered; things elsewhere a memory are in China a fact. The forced labour which, two thousand years ago, built the Great Wall out of countless humble lives is still recalled with hatred in the songs of the people. One may see stretches of the Grand Canal, thronged with traffic today, which were old when Roman engineers were driving roads through Britain; and, save that they are armed with European rifles, the bandits whose exploits fill the columns of the Press are the bandits of

Chinese novels and plays of the age of Robin Hood. China, as an organised community, with a distinctive culture, was in the past the contemporary of Egypt and Mesopotamia. In spite of recurrent invasions, civil wars, and anarchy, the vast arch of her history spans, with majestic continuity, what in the West are regarded as separate epochs. The first duty of the visitor is to remember these truisms. It is to clear his mind of the optical illusion produced by Shanghai, which eighty years ago was a mud-flat and today is a gate into China, not China herself.

That is the background of the picture, which only the ingenuous or mercenary are likely to forget. The foreground is in violent contrast with it. Isolated by geography, and with a surprisingly homogeneous civilisation in the immense range of her territory, China felt, till the nineteenth century, neither the external pressure which in Europe shaped the State, nor the rivalry of numerous independent centres of energy which was a principal stimulus to economic progress. She did not advance on all fronts at once, but was both mature and retarded. Precocious in culture, she was scantily equipped with the material organisation which is the hard shell that protects it. Her intellectual and artistic achievements were on one plane, her economic and political system on another.

The dam stood so long that the current, when it broke, was too swift to be manageable. Economic, political, and intellectual movements, which elsewhere made their way by small increments of growth, are, in the China of today, in simultaneous ferment. The literary renaissance; the attempt to create a sovereign unitary State, and its struggle against local particularism and centrifugal ambitions; the beginnings, on the eastern seaboard and the rivers, of an industrial revolution, with the criticisms and aspirations that are its natural accompaniment; the reform of local government, of education, and of the complicated structure of Chinese jurisprudence; the partial dissolution of the venerable institution of the Chinese family, with the whole system of personal responsibilities and social relations of which it was the centre—all these, and much else, have been crowded into a space of barely thirty years. It is as though Europe had passed, unprepared by an intervening discipline, from the fifteenth century to the twentieth.

The psychology of the generation now active in education

and public affairs—its nationalism, its faith in the omnipotence
of mechanism and technique, its sense of futility and recurrent
fits of depression—is the natural consequence. It is the result
of the contrast between a great cultural heritage and material
weakness. The attitude, as of tourists in Peiping, which
rhapsodises over the old China but patronises the new, very
properly exasperates it. Its eyes are on the future, not on the
past, and it allows priceless monuments, like the Ming tombs
and the Temple of Heaven, to crumble unregarded. It feels
that the salvation of its country depends on accomplishing
in a decade the work of centuries.

II

"You must see the lions." "What lions?" "The lions of the
princes of Liang."

I am no great lover of the king of beasts. The lions of my own
country—the architectural ones, I mean—provoke me to
exasperation. That insufferable air of dignified stupidity, of
tranquil, self-righteous materialism, as of a dull, rich man
staring, with stony superciliousness, over the contemptible
heads of the wretched herd of lesser beings—how cruel a
caricature! And how like us at our worst! Nor have I been
reconciled to the breed by the diminutive, goggle-eyed lions
which brandish feathery tails and wrinkle peevish noses outside
Chinese public buildings, all simper and snarl, like spoiled
King Charles's spaniels. When entering those respectable
portals, dedicated to the austere muses of statistics and law, it
is all I can do to resist startling the sentry into turning out the
guard and arresting me as a Communist by chucking the
lapdogs under their pretty little chins and exclaiming "Paid
for!"

All the same, if the lions were a bore, there was a promise of
compensations. We should leave the town by the gate which
wise builders of the past, remembering the mutability of mortal
things, and the need of providing exits from awkward situations, named the Gate of Escape. We should go round the
foot of the Purple Mountain, swarming with ghosts, where
the Host of Heavenly Peace, which cost China—so historians
say—20,000,000 lives, held its camp for ten years against the

abominable city. We should pass the tomb with a vast stone tortoise, the symbol of eternity, amid its grove of trees.

Moreover, on consulting a book by a man of learning, I saw that the lions were described, not only as lions, but also as chimeras, and that one of these chimeras was over six feet high at the shoulder. Though not without some experience, both friendly and hostile, of the great family of chimeras, I had never run one to earth before, or taken its measurements. In the end I accepted the invitation to visit the creatures with the effusive enthusiasm of inward reluctance.

Half the charm of Chinese monuments, as of those of Italy, or at least of such parts of Italy as have not been improved out of recognition, is that they stand where they were put. They are where their makers meant them to be, unclassified, uncatalogued, and unfenced, not isolated in museums from the chances of mortality. Those in the palace at Peiping are, no doubt, an exception. But even in the labels describing these, or at least in the English versions of them, there is a kind of royal amateurishness, "wielding its pen," as Scott said of Byron, "with the negligent ease of a man of quality," as though the experiment of collecting pottery and jewels behind glass for the edification of visitors were novel and uncertain.

Most of the rest were intended to live in the open air, and have continued to live in it. They have endured wind, rain, and snow; famine, banditry, revolution, and civil war; the fever of revolt, the shame of defeat, the violence of conquerors. As unchanging as the landscape of which they are part, or changing only with it, they have suffered what has been suffered by the generations around them. When they vanish, as in time they do, it is not that they have been removed, but that they are worn out and fade away, in the manner of human beings. Frost splits them, or a plant pushes its way through the stones, and a peasant picks up the fragment to be a landmark for the neighbouring scrap of land, of the size of a tablecloth, which he calls his field. No official asks what has become of them. It is natural that stones, like men, should die.

That is true even of the great monuments, which are among the wonders of the world. It is true even of the Ming tombs. The wild hills behind, the broken bridge in front, the row of gigantic sepulchres, as vast as palaces, built at regular intervals

against the steep side of the long, wooded valley where the
geomancer found that the spirits were propitious, and gleaming
ever more enormous, amid their curtain of dark trees, as one
advances towards them down the avenue of stone warriors and
beasts, strike comment silent. But the walls are sagging, and
the visitor walks round them ankle-deep in yellow tiles that
have fallen from the roofs. Fifty years hence, if decay goes on,
they will be shapeless mounds.

The lesser relics are a different story. Their very position is
sometimes only half known, except to the learned. One asks a
villager, and he asks another, and there is a hurried consultation. There is no going this way, for yesterday it rained, and
the road is water-logged; or that, for the bridge is down. It is
not certain that the stones are still standing. Much has fallen
lately, and it is a long while since anyone wanted to see them.

The journey is through time as well as through space. Rural
Japan, like many parts of rural Europe, is humming with
urban progress—surfaced roads, and electric light, and motor-
cars, and artificial fertilisers. In China there is little of these
pert amenities. In the spirit of their nation, which carried one
type of economic system and social organisation to a high level
of achievement, and was not conscious, till the Western barbarians broke in, of the need to improve or supersede it,
Chinese peasants ploughed with iron when the West used
wood, and continue to plough with it when the West uses
steel. The town, for all its antiquated traits, lives in one age,
the country in another. As in the Europe of the Middle Ages,
the townsman fears and despises the uncouth countryman; the
countryman dislikes the townsman and suspects his sharp
ways. The walls of the city are not new; they were completed,
twenty-two miles of them, in the fourteenth century. But to the
peasants they still seem, except for the refuge that they offer in
war, a modern evil, sheltering usurers, officials, and other
enemies of common men.

As we left them we mingled with the crowd engaged in the
great daily exchange, the pulse of economic life which beats
once every twenty-four hours. One long stream of villagers was
carrying into the city grass cut on the hills to serve as fuel to
cook food; for, coal being costly, the provision of warmth is
the business of the agriculturist, not the miner, and grass is

burned which in Europe would be fed to cattle or broken up
by the plough. Another stream was carrying out of it the night-
soil to fertilise the land to grow the food which the fuel would
cook. Our car became entangled in the labyrinth of a village,
ran up a hill and could go no farther, ran back and crept over a
tiny bridge with infinite precautions, and, after sidling across
the playground of a school, proceeded pretty calmly for a mile
and stopped. The road had not come to any end, but it did not
go on; probably the men who worked on it had got sick of the
job. We walked four miles between rice-fields. Then we saw
the lion.

As a matter of fact there were several, the remains of a herd,
drove, pack, or what ancient authorities on the chase called, I
believe, "a pride of lions"—part of an avenue leading to the
tomb, now lost, of a prince of the fifth century. But, such is the
effect of perfection when one meets it, we could see only one.
It filled the landscape.

Its left foot was advanced. Its shoulders and haunches were
thrown back, as though it had suddenly checked itself in a
charge. Its head was up, and the curve of its neck was like a
wave about to break. The huts of a hamlet had pushed to
within a few yards of its paws, and someone had hung a mat on
it to dry. But houses, human beings, and hills seemed suddenly
to have become small. It was like the war-horse of Job turned
into stone.

We crept away, and ate our food out of sight of it. The
children watched us, and then collected the scraps of paper for
their parents to burn, for fuel was scarce in the village.

III

To look over a plain in China from a low hill or city wall is
to see fifty villages at once. They are as thick on the ground as
are, in Western countries, individual farms. Statistics of
Chinese economic life are unreliable, but it is probable that not
less than seventy per cent of a population of something between
400,000,000 and 450,000,000 lives by agriculture. Not the
wage-earner, but the land-holding peasant, is the representative
figure in China; and, as industrialism develops, it will be from
the peasant families of today, with the standard of life to

which farm work has habituated them, that the industrial wage-earners will be drawn. Though she possesses important manufacturing industries, China is overwhelmingly a nation of farmers. Her social organisation, her culture, her economic and political problems take their colour from that fact. They are those, not of an industrial, but of an agricultural, civilisation.

It is a civilisation as yet almost untouched by the economic changes and social reforms which, between the latter part of the eighteenth century and the beginning of the twentieth, reconstructed the agriculture and land system of Europe. Neither biology and chemistry, nor mechanical transport, nor enclosure and consolidation, nor the reform of land tenure, nor co-operative marketing and credit have as yet, save in a few exceptional areas, begun to affect it. Chinese methods of cultivation have been held up to admiration by Western observers, and, as a triumph of individual skill and industry, unaided by organised knowledge, their reputation is deserved. But it is the agriculture of a pre-scientific age, which perpetuates a venerable tradition and rarely improves on it. Though it has become a convention to describe it as intensive, the word is misleading. Intensive in its use of labour, Chinese farming is unintensive in the inadequacy of the equipment by which labour is assisted. It produces an output per acre, which, in the case of one crop, rice, is surprisingly high, but its output per worker is invariably low, and it conserves the fertility of the soil—its special boast—at the cost of exploiting the human beings who till it. Judged by the standards of the West, it is at once under-capitalised and over-manned.

The fact which determines its character is the tiny size of most holdings, which in turn is the result of a pressure of population so intense that in certain considerable areas the number of human beings per square mile of cultivated land exceeds 2,000. If official figures may be trusted, a third of the farms are under one-and-a-half acres, and approximately one-half under four acres. The tiny patches separated by baulks, which diversify the vast and solemn landscape of great parts of China, give the impression of an agriculture of pygmies in a land of giants. Not only does the sub-division of farms among heirs produce a continuous *morcellement* of land, but, as in Europe before enclosure, in the unenclosed parts of it today,

and in India and Japan, those in a single tenure do not lie on a
compact block, but are composed of anything from five to
fifteen separate parcels scattered over hedgeless fields.

The prevalence of minute holdings has necessitated special
methods of cultivation to make them yield a livelihood, and
these methods, in turn, involving as they do intense application and much heavy physical labour, are of a kind which can
be practised only when holdings are minute. While a generalised
picture is necessarily misleading, the common factor, which
gives the methods of different parts of the country such unity
as they possess, is the necessity, since land is scarce, of squeezing
the last drop of nutriment out of such land as there is. The
result is an agriculture which has been aptly described as a
kind of gardening.

In such conditions, standards of life are inevitably low, and
the margin which separates peasant families from hunger uncertain and narrow. Such margin as exists is further reduced
by the character of the social environment in which farming is
carried on. All the evils which, till less than a century and a
half ago, made the social problem of most parts of Europe, not
the urban wage-earner, but the peasant, exist today in China
in an aggravated form.

Communications so intolerable as to cause the roads cursed
by Arthur Young to seem a miracle of efficiency make the cost
of moving crops almost prohibitive. As a result, there is a
multitude of tiny local markets in which prices fluctuate
violently, and, while consumers in one region are threatened
with famine, farmers are ruined in another because they cannot dispose of their surplus. Owing to lack of reserves they
must sell immediately after harvest when prices are falling, and
are an easy prey to the local monopolist; a good deal of what
passes under the name of trade appears to consist, indeed, of
the practices which a less polite age called forestalling and
regrating. No organised machinery exists to finance agriculture. Hence the peasant gets credit where he can, when he
can, and on what terms he can, and, since his necessities are
desperate, is often skinned alive. Money-lending in China can
be described only by the medieval phrase, *vorago iniquitatis*.
Interest at twenty-five to fifty per cent is common; interest at
fifty to one hundred per cent is not unknown. As far as the

poorer peasants are concerned, permanent indebtedness is the rule rather than the exception. They pawn their crops in summer, their farm implements in winter, and their household belongings throughout the whole twelve months.

Though the question of land-tenure is a less burning issue than it was during certain periods in the history of Europe, it is in parts of China sufficiently serious. She possesses, it is true, no landed aristocracy, no dominant class of junker or squires, and few beasts. Manorial estates, if they ever existed, have left few traces, and, since animal husbandry is of minor importance, the conflict over common pastures and meadows, which kept European villages simmering for the greater part of a thousand years, presents no problem. But, while in the north occupying owners form, perhaps, three-quarters of the farming population, in the south, where tenancy predominates, there are bitter and just complaints of over-renting and of the tyranny of landlords. Nor are such conditions confined to one region alone. The investigations of Professor J. L. Buck, the leading authority on the subject, have shown that in north and east-central China, where land-tenure is less commercialised than in the south, the proportion of his total receipts paid by the farmer to the landlord is altogether excessive.

The poverty arising from primitive economic methods and defective organisation is aggravated by political disorder. It is easy to exaggerate it, but it is true that the rural population, in certain parts of the country, suffers horribly through the insecurity of life and property. It is taxed by one ruffian who calls himself a general, by a second, by a third; in some places actually more than twenty years' taxation have been paid in advance. It is compelled to cut its crops at the point of the bayonet and hand them over without payment to the local military commander, though it will starve without them. It pays blackmail to the professional bandits in its neighbourhood; or it resists, and a year later, when the bandits have assumed uniform, sees its village burned to the ground. When human enemies are absent the farmer must still reckon with a remorseless nature. "What drove you to settle here, so far from home?" we asked a peasant. The reply was, "Bandits, soldiers, and famine." But famine, though the feature of Chinese economic life of which the West hears most, is merely the last stage of a disease which is always present. There are parts of the country in which the rural population is like a man standing up to his neck in water. A ripple is sufficient to drown it.

The condition of the peasant, though it attracts less attention than that of the factory worker, is far the gravest of the problems with which China is confronted. The Ministries concerned announced a long series of measures in the spring of 1930. As far as programmes are in question, all the reforms carried out in other parts of the world in the course of the last century are now part of the official policy of the Republic. The matters on which action is most urgent are not difficult to determine. Transport is crucial. The farmer has no incentive to increase his output if he cannot be certain of disposing of it, and the recurrence of local famines is inevitable as long as it is impossible to relieve the deficiency of one area by the surplus of another. In agriculture, as in manufacturing industry, and, indeed in government and administration, an improvement in the means of communication is the indispensable condition of all other reforms. Those entitled to an opinion are agreed that the technique of farming can be greatly improved by the use of modern knowledge. Universities and the State, in their different ways, are labouring to improve it. But the introduction of better methods depends, not merely on the research work of scientific and governmental institutions, but on the degree to which its results are disseminated among those who must apply them in practice. Out of a population of over 400,000,000 probably not more than 20,000,000 are in schools of any kind, and, until primary education is far more widely diffused than is the case today, the new possibilities cannot easily be made accessible to the rural population. Co-operative credit and marketing have in the course of little more than three-quarters of a century done much to deliver the European peasant from his immemorial servitude to the usurer and middleman. In China they are in their infancy; the first credit society was established in 1922, and probably not more than 700 to 800 are in existence today. The movement has, however, begun, with the encouragement of national and provincial authorities, and in time, it may reasonably be hoped, will not only improve the economic position of the peasants but give them, as the result of organisation, a new weight in public affairs. Except

where, as in certain provinces, tenants have taken the law into
their own hands, next to nothing has been done to improve
conditions of land tenure. The official policy—the establishment of tribunals to revise rents downwards—is by itself
inadequate. Nor has machinery yet been created to give even it
effect.

IV

The seven months since September 1930, have been the
first breathing-space since the Nationalist Government established itself. Every week that elapses without war makes less
probable the recurrence of war, but peace is still a fragile plant.
The question is whether it will continue long enough for the
forces on the side of unity and order to become too strong to be
overthrown, as so often in the past, by those making for anarchy
and disintegration.

Both are powerful, and the difficulty is to strike a balance
between them. Perhaps, indeed, to strike a balance is not
merely difficult, but impossible; the country is so vast, the
interests involved so diverse and complex, the absence of the
settled forms and habits of political procedure which canalise
action elsewhere so conducive to abrupt deviations and unpre-
dictable eruptions. Political forces in China recall Chinese
rivers. The pressure on the dam is enormous, but unseen, and
it is not till it bursts that the strain is realised. The visitor commonly miscalculates the violence of the current, with the result
that he underestimates the magnitude of the difficulties con-
fronting governments, and does less than justice to the efforts
made to overcome them. Then, if he is prudent, he takes a
map; goes through the provinces one by one; tries to visualise
the existence of their inhabitants; marks with a pencil those
where the authority of Nanking is effective, those where it is
nominal, those where it is openly defied, those where it is
hardly known. His perspective changes. The capital dwindles
to one city in a continent partly friendly, partly indifferent,
partly hostile. It is France in the twelfth century on a scale
immensely greater—Paris and the Île de France, a little circle
of light, in one corner of it, and for the rest a welter of liberties.

That, no doubt, is an exaggeration, but it is part of the
picture. The first problem, which lies behind all questions of

particular reforms, is vast and fundamental. It is not who shall
govern the State, but whether there shall be a State at all. It is
whether public power shall exist. China has known no Roman
Empire. The idea of a sovereign, of an even pressure of law, of
the impersonal majesty of an authority to which, and not to his
family and his friends, the individual owes allegiance, of the
Res publica, which in Europe men remembered dimly when all
had slipped and struggled back to as to a rock—that idea is
not an ancient part of the nation's mental furniture, but a
modern growth, which struggles feebly for life amid interests
and sentiments that overshadow and strangle it. The thought
of China, one and indivisible, is, no doubt, a power. But it is
commonly the reflection of a great cultural tradition. As a
political force, expressed in habits and institutions, it still has
to be created.

The relations between Nanking and the north, where the
young marshal, with the interests and resources of Manchuria
behind him, rules somewhere down to the region of the Yellow
River, is one example of that phenomenon. It would be crude,
no doubt, to describe them as international; but, as long as
troops are commanded, and part of the taxes levied, in his
name, are they domestic? The quasi-independence of the
generals in certain provinces is another. Some of them, it is
fair to say, have built roads—a strand in the rope that one day,
it may be hoped, will hang them. For the rest, they appear to
be common tyrants, of a type of which the past history of
Europe offers sufficient examples, who raise private armies,
grind the faces of the poor with private taxes, and wage, when
they fall out with each other, private wars. The disposition,
revealed once more in the last few weeks, to regard the threat
of revolt as the natural form of political demonstration is a
third phenomenon of the same type. The existence of small
enclaves where the writ of Nanking does not run and where
such government as exists is commonly, if inaccurately, said to
be carried on by Communists, as in Kiangsi, Fukien, and
Hunan, is a fourth. The prevalence of banditry is a fifth. A
sixth is the fact that in part of the country the peasants, driven
to desperation, have armed and formed leagues to keep out
"bandits, Communists, and Government soldiers."

The word Communism, it is true, is used in the China of

1931 even more loosely than elsewhere. In reality, whatever the future may contain, though economic discontent is given a doctrinal edge by political tacticians, the so-called Communist question is still very largely a land question. It is most acute where the proportion of tenants among farmers is highest, and where the conditions of tenure are worst. In such regions, much that the Press ascribes to Communist machinations appears to a Western observer to have at present as much, or as little, to do with theoretical Communism as the Peasants' Revolt of 1381 in England or the *Jacquerie* in France, and the military measures invoked to suppress them as inappropriate as a surgical operation to a patient dying of consumption. Here again, however, the significant fact is that the forces are centrifugal. "What do you know of the National Government?" a peasant was asked. "Nothing." "Of the Provincial Government?" "Nothing." "Of the government of the district?" "Nothing." "Of the village gentry?" "They count for something."

Nor is a psychology to which personal loyalties are everything and the State nothing peculiar to the village. It emerges, with the inevitability of an automatic reaction, in quarters where its survival would be least expected. A mild, spectacled reformer will discuss the desirability of giving a more progressive turn to the Government's policy. Asked how he proposes to achieve that result, "Oh," he answers, "there are X and Y, and other oppressed generals. They will take a hand in the business." You discover that he is banking on a war of dissatisfied *condottieri*. The material conditions which fixed such habits of mind still continue to reinforce them. Banditry is largely, if not wholly, an economic phenomenon, a sign that, with the pressure on the land, the lower strata of rural society are crumbling. Financial stringency causes military commanders to be allowed to live on the country, with the result that they and their troops are potential rebels. In most countries modern weapons, being costly to acquire and requiring some technical skill for their use, have strengthened governments against revolt. In China they sometimes seem to have produced the opposite result. They make it difficult for the rural population to deal with its local tyrants as they deserve; while, owing to lack of communications, the superior resources of the State cannot easily be mobilised against them in over-whelming force.

Such phenomena explain the despondency which sometimes distresses a foreigner in his Chinese friends. There is a profound sense of the need for reconstruction and an admirable energy in labouring at plans to promote it. Then the ground shifts and everything seems to be again about to crumble. Military costs and the service of the debt absorb so large a proportion of the national revenue that constructive effort is paralysed. Intelligence and public spirit have so often been stultified by political instability that the most courageous and devoted are tempted to exclaim, "Who shall show us any good!" But there are lights in the picture as well as shadows. The programme of the revolution was not merely to overthrow a system of government, but to create a State and to modernise economic organisation. If the pace of the movement has not been that expected, its direction has as yet been kept, and in matters of this kind a generation, after all, is no long period. As it is, for all its precariousness, the political situation is held by good judges to be more hopeful than at any time in the recent past. Economic development has been crippled by insecurity; but, measured by the increase in the number of industrial enterprises, it has continued more steadily in the past ten years than, in view of the unfavourable environment, might have been expected. If only peace can be maintained, political stability will hasten economic progress, and economic progress will in turn reinforce political stability.

As far as material requirements are concerned, the indispensable condition of both is the same. It is an immediate and continuous improvement in the means of communication, without which political unity must remain a mere phrase. It is to the extension of railways, as finance makes it possible, and the mobilisation of all available labour for the construction of roads, which in a country congested with soldiers is possible at once, that resources and intelligence need first to be devoted. The second essential is a serious attack on the land question. Chinese society is crumbling at the bottom. No stable political system can be built on such foundations. The peasants today seem helpless; but the State rests on their shoulders. Unless it provides them, as at present it does not, with practical reasons for supporting it, they will not bear the load for ever.[1] A fact, in the third place, less often realised, but almost equally important, is the clog on the national energies imposed by the absence of any comprehensive system of public education. It is all very well to talk eloquently about modernisation; but one cannot have modern industry without modern engineers, or modern farming without modern farmers, or a modern State without modern citizens. Nor can any of these essentials exist as long as from half to three-quarters of the rising generation has no opportunity of systematic training and there is no easy circulation of ideas to break down rural isolation and create a consciousness of common interests. The fourth conclusion which impresses itself on an outside observer is the dangerous futility of the policy of repression pursued by the Government. A drastic censorship, the virtual prohibition of political discussion, the refusal to respect the personal liberty of political opponents, an atrocious brutality in inflicting punishments, up to death itself, on persons, including mere boys, accused of anti-government propaganda—such policies are signs, not of strength, but of feebleness. The weakest point of the present regime is its isolation. It is its failure, in spite of some genuine services rendered by it, to establish cordial relations with any strong body of social forces, and the air of a personal or family arrangement backed by military force which as a consequence clings to it. Few at present desire its fall, for the alternative to it is anarchy; but fewer still feel the enthusiasm for it which three years ago brought it to power. If it is to stand, it must rest on an altogether broader basis of public confidence. And only they can enjoy the advantage of public support who will submit to the inconvenience of public criticism.

[1] The measures required are indicated in the author's *Land and Labour in China* (Allen & Unwin, 1932). Some of them appear at last to have been taken.

5

The Choice before the Labour Party[1]

I

Now that the dust has settled, it is possible to examine the landscape left by the earthquake. The election of 1931 was, by general consent, a considerable sensation. But neither the preliminary manœuvres of the kind described by Lord Passfield in the *Political Quarterly*, nor the methods adopted during the contest itself, are the phenomena on which today it is most profitable for a member of the Labour Party to reflect. Political coroners may sit on the corpse of the late Cabinet, but the ordinary citizen is more concerned with its behaviour before life was extinct. What matters to him, and what is likely to determine his attitude when next the Labour Party appeals for his support, is less the question of the circumstances in which the last Government went out, than that of what it did, attempted, and neither did nor attempted to do, when it was in. It is possible that his verdict on its death, if at this time of day he paused to consider it, would be neither murder nor misadventure, but pernicious anaemia producing general futility.

For the events of the summer of 1931 were the occasion, rather than the cause, of the *débâcle* of the Labour Party. In spite of the dramatic episodes which heralded its collapse, the Government did not fall with a crash, in a tornado from the blue. It crawled slowly to its doom, deflated by inches, partly

[1] 1934, published by the *Political Quarterly*. It should be needless to remark that many of the defects ascribed in this paper to the Labour Party no longer exist.

by its opponents, partly by circumstances beyond its control, but partly also by itself. The gunpowder was running out of it from the moment it assumed office, and was discovered, on inspection, to be surprisingly like sawdust. Due allowance must be made, no doubt, for the cruel chance which condemned it to face the worst collapse in prices of modern history; and due credit must be given for the measures which it introduced, but failed, through no fault of its own, to pass into law. But, granted the inexorable limits, can it seriously be argued that it was audacious in working up to them?

The commonest answer to that question was given in two words: minority government. To the writer it appeared at the time, and appears today, unconvincing. When the Cabinet took office, two alternatives were open to it. It could decide to live dangerously, or to play for safety. It could choose a short life, and—if the expression be not too harsh—an honest one; or it could proceed on the assumption that, once a Labour Government is in office, its primary duty is to find means of remaining there. If it acted on its principles, it could not hope to survive for more than twelve months. It could postpone its execution, but only at the cost of making its opponents the censors of its policy. It would invite them, in effect, to decide the character of the measures which it should be permitted to introduce, and to determine the issues of the next election.

The Labour Government of 1929–31 chose the second course. It chose it, it must in fairness be admitted, with the tacit approval of the great majority of the party, including, as far as is known, those trade-union elements in it which afterwards revolted against the results of the decision. The effects of its choice were, however, serious. Parts in life, once adopted, develop their consequences with a logic of their own, overriding the volition of the actors cast for them; however repulsive, if played at all, they must be played with gusto. Once convinced that discretion was their cue, ministers brought to the practice of the golden mean a conscientious assiduity almost painful to contemplate. They threw themselves into the role of *The Obsequious Apprentice, or Prudence Rewarded,* as though bent on proving that, so far from being different from other governments, His Majesty's Labour Government could rival the most respectable of them in cautious conventionality.

Industrial and social reconstruction, the favourite theme of Labour orators, owed little to the existence of a Labour Cabinet. The Government doubtless felt itself precluded, till the Macmillan Committee had reported, from making up its mind on the questions of currency and credit which were to prove its undoing. Even in matters, however, where delay was not imposed by circumstances, its action did not err on the side of trenchancy. It found coal, cotton, and steel with one foot in the nineteenth century; it left them there. What passed in its inner councils is, of course, unknown, but it gave few outward symptoms of realising that, if the modernisation of the major industries is to be handled at all, it must be planned as a whole, or of grasping the necessity of creating a permanent organ to press it steadily forward, or of appreciating the importance of devoting attention to the long-range aspects of unemployment, as distinct from monthly fluctuations in the number of unemployed. It had even to be stimulated by the protests of its followers in the House into proceeding—too late—with its little Education Bill. In one sphere, indeed, that of international policy, it achieved, in the opinion of good judges, solid and genuine successes. Apart from that important exception, and from the fact that, if King Log was bad, King Stork would be worse, what strong reason could be advanced for desiring its survival?

The degeneration of Socialist parties on assuming office is now an old story. If it is worth while to recall the latest British version of it, it is not in order to visit on individuals collective shortcomings. It is because, till its lessons are learned, the wretched business will go on. If the laments of some ex-ministers at the "conspiracy," which "stabbed them in the back"—as though a Titan, all energy and ardour, had been felled at his forge by the hand of assassins—were merely undignified, they would properly be ignored. Unfortunately, they are worse. What Labour most needs is not self-commiseration, but a little cold realism. These plaintive romancers would dry its tears with a tale of Red Riding Hood and the wicked wolf. They retard the recovery of the party by concealing its malady. They perpetuate the mentality which requires to be overcome before recovery can take place. The sole cure for its disease is sincerity. They offer it scape-goats.

If it is sincere, it will not be drugged by these opiates. It will not soothe the pain of defeat with the flattering illusion that it is the innocent victim of faults not its own. It is nothing of the kind. It is the author, the unintending and pitiable author, of its own misfortunes. It made a government in its own image; and the collapse of that government was the result neither of accident—though that played its part—nor of unfavourable circumstances—though luck was against it—nor, least of all, it must be repeated, of merely personal failings. It was in the logic of history; for 1929–31 repeated 1924. It sprang from within, not without; for it had begun within six months of the Government's return, and the flight from principles was both earlier and more precipitate than the flight from the pound. It was the consequence, not of individual defects, but of a general habit of mind and outlook on affairs which ministers had acquired long before they could anticipate that power would be their lot. What was tried, and found wanting, was, in short, not merely two years of a Labour Cabinet, but a decade of Labour politics.

Such, and not merely the events of a few weeks in the summer of 1931, were the cause of the *débâcle*. If these are the realities, to make the conduct of individuals, however odious in itself, the main target of criticism is to exaggerate their importance. To expel a person is not to exorcise a spirit. The truth is simpler and more serious. In the swift growth of the Labour Movement since 1918, its inner flaws had been concealed. But they had not disappeared; some of them, indeed, had deepened. At the moment when the reality of power seemed almost within its grasp, its old faults found it out. It now has an interval in which to meditate its errors.

II

The gravest weakness of British Labour is one which it shares with the greater part of the world, including British capitalists. It is its lack of a creed. The Labour Party is hesitant in action, because divided in mind. It does not achieve what it could, because it does not know what it wants. It frets out of office and fumbles in it, because it lacks the assurance either to wait or to strike. Being without clear convictions as to its own meaning

and purpose, it is deprived of the dynamic which only convictions can supply. If it neither acts with decision nor
inspires others so to act, the principal reason is that it is itself
undecided.

This weakness is fundamental. If it continues uncorrected,
there neither is, nor ought to be, a future for the Labour
Party. A political creed, it need hardly be said, is neither a
system of transcendental doctrines nor a code of rigid formulae.
It is a common conception of the ends of political action, and
of the means of achieving them, based on a common view of
the life proper to human beings, and of the steps required at
any moment more nearly to attain it. A movement, like an
individual, cannot build its existence round an internal
vacuum. Till the void in the mind of the Labour Party is
filled—till interests are hammered by principles into a serviceable tool, which is what interests should be, and a steady will
for a new social order takes the place of mild yearnings to make
somewhat more comfortable terms with the social order of
today—mere repairs to the engines will produce little but
disillusionment.

There is much criticism at the moment of organisation and
programmes. Some of it, like that which ascribes the troubles
of the party to its trade union connections, is misconceived. It
is obvious that the unions, like other elements in English
society, including the intelligentsia, are most imperfectly
socialised. It is obvious that the weight which is given them at
party conferences by the card vote is an anomaly, which has a
historical justification, but is not permanently defensible. The
picture, however, of torpid and rapacious trade unionists
impeding bold schemes of constructive statesmanship is a
caricature; it cannot truly be said that the late Government
was harassed by recurrent pressure to sacrifice the larger aims
of the movement to the sectional interests of one element in it.
Some of the criticism, again, like the recoil of some members of
the party from the social services—as though to recognise
unemployment pay for the sorry makeshift it is involved repudiating the communism of Public Health, Housing and Education—is a mood of reaction, engendered by defeat, which in
time will pass. But much of it is justified. The only comment to
be made on it is that it does not go far enough.

Of course the programme of the party needs to be modernised; of course its organisation requires to be overhauled. No one who knows how the former is made and the latter works is likely to remain long on his knees before either. But, granted the obvious weaknesses of both—granted the intellectual timidity, conservatism, conventionality, which keeps policy trailing tardily in the rear of realities, and over which, if one's taste is for brilliance on the cheap, it is so easy to make merry—the root of the matter is elsewhere. These defects are the symptoms, not the source, of the trouble. They are, not causes, but effects.

The characteristic vice of the programmes of the party, as set out in conference resolutions, is that too often they are not programmes. They sweep together great things and small; nationalise land, mines and banking in one sentence, and abolish fox-hunting in the next; and, by touching on everything, commit ministers to nothing. The characteristic defect of its practical procedure is its tendency to rely for success on the mass support of societies, and the mass vote of constituencies, of whom neither have been genuinely converted to its principles. It requires an army. It collects a mob. The mob disperses. That is the nature of mobs.

But why are Labour programmes less programmes than miscellanies—a glittering forest of Christmas trees, with presents for everyone, instead of a plan of campaign for what must be, on any showing, a pretty desperate business? Because the party is at present without any ordered conception of the task. Because it possesses in its own mind nothing analogous to what used to be called, in the days when it was necessary to put jobs through to time, a scheme of priorities. Because it has no stable standard of political values, such as would teach it to discriminate between the relative urgency of different objectives. Because, lacking such a standard, it lacks also the ability to subordinate the claims of different sections of the movement to the progress of the whole, and to throw its whole weight against the central positions, where success means something, and failure itself is not wholly a disaster, instead of frittering away its *moral* in inconclusive skirmishes.

And why is the Labour Party's organisation, in spite of its admirable *personnel*, stronger in numbers than in quality? For precisely the same reason. Because the finest individuals are nothing till mastered by a cause. Because the party, being itself not too certain what that cause is, has found it difficult to present it in a form convincing to plain men, of whom the majority, in England, as elsewhere, are not politicians. Because, instead of stating its faith, undiluted and unqualified, and waiting for their support till, with the teaching of experience, which today teaches pretty fast, they come to share it, it tried to buy their votes with promises, whether they shared that faith or not. Because it appealed to them, on the ground, not that a Labour Government would be different from other governments, but that it would be a worthy successor to all British governments that had ever been. Because, when it ought to have called them to a long and arduous struggle, it too often did the opposite. It courted them with hopes of cheaply won benefits, and, if it did not despise them, sometimes addressed them as though it did. It demanded too little, and offered too much. It assured them that its aim was the supersession of capitalism, but that, in the meantime, the two-hooped pot should have four hoops. Is it surprising if they concluded that, since capitalism was the order of the day, it had better continue to be administered by capitalists, who, at any rate—so, poor innocents, they supposed—knew how to make the thing work?

These, it will be replied, are hard sayings. They are; but, unfortunately, they are true. The inner state of the movement has been concealed from itself by the glamour of a word. That word is Socialism. In 1918, the Labour Party finally declared itself to be a Socialist Party. It supposed, and supposes, that it thereby became one. It is mistaken. It recorded a wish, that is all; the wish has not been fulfilled. If it now disciplines itself for a decade, it may become a Socialist Party. It is not one at present. Until it recognises that it is not Socialist, it is not likely to become Socialist.

Like any other creed, Socialism has two aspects. It implies a personal attitude and a collective effort. The quality of the latter depends on the sincerity of the former. The collective effort involves three essentials: agreement as to the kind of society which it is desired to establish; agreement as to the nature of the resistance to be overcome in establishing it; agreement as to the technique, the methods and machinery, required for its establishment. The history of British Socialism, during the present century, is largely the story of the concentration of attention on the third requirement, to the neglect of the two first.

The effort devoted to questions of method has, in itself, been admirable. But expedients require, in order that they may be applied, and produce, when applied, the results intended, a situation in which their application, their continuous application on a large scale, is possible. Such a situation can exist only if Socialists come to power, not as diffident agents of policies not their own, but as Socialists, and, having done so, are prepared to deal with the opposition which they will encounter. They must have created behind them, before they assume office, a strong body of opinion, which "knows what it fights for, and loves what it knows." They must have measured coolly the forces which will be mobilised against them. The Labour Party has done neither.

The reasons are partly historical. The British Labour Movement was offered in its youth a foreign, and peculiarly arid, version of Marxian Socialism. It very sensibly rejected it. Then the unexpected happened. The seed sown by the pioneers began to bear fruit. The movement became a political power. Whole battalions were shepherded into it, much as the troops of Feng-Yu-Hsiang, "the Christian general," were baptised with a hose. Thanks to the judges, the unions were the first wave. The war brought another; the election of 1923 a third; the events of 1926 a fourth. By that time a generation had grown up to which it seemed as easy to be a Socialist—as easy, if you please!—as it had seemed difficult in 1900.

The result was that the British Labour Party, like British industry, was for a time too prosperous. It behaved, as the latter had behaved, as though summer would last for ever. It had inherited from the nineteenth century the economic psychology of an age of expansion. In the flush of success, its political psychology assumed for a time the same florid complexion. It deceived itself both as to its own condition, and as to the character of the forces on its side and against it. It mistook luck for merit; treated votes, which were clearly indispensable, as equivalent to convictions, as to the practical value of which it was not equally certain; and drugged itself with the illusion that, by adding one to one, it would achieve

the millennium, without the painful necessity of clarifying its
mind, disciplining its appetites, and training for a tough
wrestle with established power and property. It touched
lightly on its objectives, or veiled them in the radiant ambiguity
of the word Socialism, which each hearer could interpret to
his taste. So it ended by forgetting the reason for its existence.
It has now to rediscover it.

Yet the objective of a Socialist Party, and of the Labour
Party in so far as it deserves the name, is simplicity itself.
The fundamental question, as always, is: Who is to be master?
Is the reality behind the decorous drapery of political democracy
to continue to be the economic power wielded by a few thousand
—or, if that be preferred, a few hundred thousand—bankers,
industrialists, and landowners? Or shall a serious effort be made
—as serious, for example, as was made, for other purposes,
during the war—to create organs through which the nation can
control, in co-operation with other nations, its economic
destinies; plan its business as it deems most conducive to the
general well-being; override, for the sake of economic efficiency,
the obstruction of vested interests; and distribute the product
of its labours in accordance with some generally recognised
principles of justice? Capitalist parties presumably accept the
first alternative. A Socialist Party chooses the second. The
nature of its business is determined by its choice.

The business is not the passage of a series of reforms in the
interests of different sections of the working classes. It is to
abolish all advantages and disabilities which have their source,
not in differences of personal quality, but in disparities of
wealth, opportunity, social position, and economic power. It
is, in short—it is absurd that at this time of day the statement
should be necessary—a classless society, which does not mean
a society without differentiated groups, but one in which
varieties of individual endowment, not contrasts of property,
income and access to education, are the basis of differentiation.
It is not a question, of course, either of merely improving the
distribution of wealth, or of merely increasing its production,
but of doing both together. Naturally, the methods required
to attain that objective are various, complex, and tedious.
Naturally, those who accept it may do so for more than one
reason—because they think it more conducive to economic

efficiency than a capitalism which no longer, as in its prime, delivers the goods; or merely because they have an eccentric prejudice in favour of treating men as men; or, since the reasons are not necessarily inconsistent, for both reasons at once. In either case, they are Socialists, though on matters of technique and procedure they may be uninstructed Socialists. Those who do not accept it are not Socialists, though they may be as wise as Solon and as virtuous as Aristides. Socialism thus defined, will be unpleasant, of course, to some persons professing it. Who promised them pleasure?

The elements composing the Labour Party are extremely miscellaneous. If variety of educational experience and economic condition among its active supporters be the test, it is, whether fortunately, or not, as a mere matter of fact, less of a class party than any other British party. That variety means that the bond of common experience is weaker than in parties whose members have been taught at school and college to hang together. Hence it makes the cohesion which springs from common intellectual convictions all the more indispensable. There is room for workers of all types in it, but on one condition. It is that, in their public capacity, they put their personal idiosyncracies second, and their allegiance to the objectives of the party first. If they accept titles and such toys without a clear duty to the movement to do so; or think that their main business is not fundamental reconstruction, but more money for the unemployed; or suppose that such reconstruction, instead of being specially urgent in the circumstances of today, must be kept in cold storage till the automatic occurrence of a hypothetical trade revival; or, like thirty-six Labour Members in the last House of Commons, regard the defence of the interests, or fancied interests, of denominational schools as more important than to strike a small blow at class privilege in education, they may be virtuous individuals, but they are not Socialists. To the Labour Party they are a source, not of strength, but of weakness. They widen the rift between its principles and its practice.

The programme of the party, again, covers a wide range. Nor need that be regretted, but, again, on one condition. It is that the different proposals contained in it should be rigorously subordinated to the main objective. Clearly, class privilege takes more than one form. It is both economic and social. It rests on functionless property, on the control of key-positions in finance and industry, on educational inequalities, on the mere precariousness of proletarian existence, which prevents its victims looking before and after. Clearly, therefore, a movement seeking to end class privilege must use more than one weapon; and clearly, also, the Labour Party's programme, like all Socialist programmes, from the Communist Manifesto to the present day, must include measures which are secondary as well as measures which are primary. The essential thing is that it should discriminate between them. What will not do is that a programme should be built up by a process of half-unconscious log-rolling, this measure being offered to one section of workers, and that, because no one must be left in the cold, being promised to another.

The Labour Party can be either a political agent, pressing in Parliament the claims of different groups of wage-earners; or it can be an instrument for the establishment of a Socialist Commonwealth, which alone, on its own principles, would meet those claims effectively, but would not meet them at once. What it cannot be is both at the same time in the same measure. It ought to tell its supporters that obvious truth. It ought to inform them that its business is to be the organ of a peaceful revolution, and that other interests must be subordinated to that primary duty. It is objected that, by taking that course, it will alienate many of them. It may, for the time being; New Models are not made by being all things to all men. But it will keep those worth keeping. And those retained will gather others, of a kind who will not turn back in the day of battle.

To formulate from time to time, amid swiftly changing complexities, international and domestic, a Labour policy which is relevant and up to date, is a task for the best brains that politics can command. But, when policy has been determined, two facts are as certain as political facts can be. The first is that, if a Labour Government, when it gets the opportunity, proceeds to act on it, it will encounter at once determined resistance. The second is that it will not overcome that resistance, unless it has explained its aims with complete openness and candour. It cannot avoid the struggle, except by compromising its principles; it must, therefore, prepare for it. In order to prepare for it, it must create in advance a temper and mentality of a kind to carry it through, not one crisis, but a series of crises, to which the Zinovieff letter and the Press campaign of 1931 will prove, it is to be expected, to have been mere skirmishes of outposts. Onions can be eaten leaf by leaf, but you cannot skin a live tiger paw by paw; vivisection is its trade, and it does the skinning first. If the Labour Party is to tackle its job with some hope of success, it must mobilise behind it a body of conviction as resolute and informed as the opposition in front of it.

To say this is not at all to lend countenance to a sterile propaganda of class hatred, or to forget that both duty and prudence require that necessary changes should be effected without a breakdown, or to ignore the truism that the possibility of effecting them is conditioned by international, as much as by domestic, factors. It is curious, in view of the historical origins of the Liberal Movement, and, indeed, of such recent history as the campaign of 1909 against "the peers and their litter," that Liberals, of all people, should find a rock of offence in the class connections of the Labour Party. The reason for facing with candour the obvious and regrettable fact of the existence of a class struggle is not, of course, to idolise class, but to make it less of an idol than in England, especially among the rich, it at present is. It is to dissolve a morbid complex in the only way in which complexes can be dissolved, not by suppressing, but by admitting it. It is to emphasise that the dynamic of any living movement is to be found, not merely in interests, but in principles, which unite men whose personal interests may be poles asunder, and that, if principles are to exercise their appeal, they must be frankly stated. The form which the effort to apply them assumes necessarily varies, of course, from one society to another. Any realist view of the future of British Socialism must obviously take account of the political maturity and dependence on a world economy of the people of Great Britain. It does not follow, however, that the struggle to be faced is less severe on that account. Intellectually and morally it may be more exacting.

If there is any country where the privileged classes are simpletons, it is certainly not England. The idea that tact and amiability in presenting the Labour Party's case—the "states-manship" of the last Government—can hoodwink them into the belief that it is also theirs is as hopeful as an attempt to bluff a sharp solicitor out of a property of which he holds the title-deeds. The plutocracy consists of agreeable, astute, forcible, self-confident, and, when hard-pressed, unscrupulous people, who know pretty well which side their bread is buttered, and intend that the supply of butter shall not run short. They respect success, the man or movement that "brings it off." But they have, very properly, no use for cajolery, and laugh in their sleeves—and not always in their sleeves—at attempts to wheedle them. The way to deal with them is not to pretend, as some Labour leaders do, that, because many of them are pleasant creatures, they can be talked into the belief that they want what the Labour Movement wants, and differ only as to methods. It is, except for the necessary contacts of political warfare, to leave them alone till one can talk with effect, when less talking will be needed, and, in the meantime, to seize every opportunity of forcing a battle on fundamental questions. When they have been knocked out in a straight fight on some major economic issues, they will proceed, in the words of Walt Whitman, to "re-examine philosophies and religions." They will open their eyes and mend their manners. They will not do so before. Why should they?

III

If such are the objectives of the Labour Party, and such the forces against it, what are the practical conclusions? They are four, relating respectively to programmes, propaganda, discipline, and tactics.

The conclusion of a pamphlet is not the proper place for even the outline of a policy, which, with the world sliding as it is, may be out of date in six months. But certain points are clear. The business of making programmes by including in them an assortment of measures appealing to different sections of the movement must stop. The function of the party is not to offer the largest possible number of carrots to the largest possible number of donkeys. It is, while working for international peace and co-operation abroad, to carry through at home the large measures of economic and social reconstruction which, to the grave injury of the nation, have been too long postponed, and with that object to secure that the key positions of the economic system are under public control.

That task must, of course, be interpreted in a broad sense. It is not for Labour to relapse into the philistinism of the May "economy" report, with its assumption that all but economic interests, and those interpreted à la capitalist, are of secondary importance. Side by side with action of a strictly economic character, such as the transference to public owner-ship of foundation services; the establishment of machinery to bring the supply of capital to industry under public control; the creation of a permanent Planning Department; and such other measures of the same order as may be adopted, must go a policy for the improvement of education, health, and the system of local government, which themselves, it may be remarked, are matters not irrelevant to economic prosperity. It is monstrous that services vital to the welfare of the great majority of the population, and especially to that of the young, should be crippled or curtailed, while the *rentier* takes an actually larger percentage than in the past of the national income. If that income is too small to permit of our ensuring that all children have proper opportunities of health and education, it is clearly too small to allow us other luxuries, including the continued payment of between £200,000,000 and £300,000,000 a year to holders of war debt.

Of the general considerations which arise in planning a programme, the most important are three. The essentials must be put first, and sectional claims must not be permitted to conflict with them. The transference of economic power to public hands must take precedence over the mere alleviation of distress. It must be recognised that any serious attempt to give effect to such a policy will provoke a counter-attack, including action to cause economic embarrassment to the Government of the day, and measures to meet it must be prepared in advance. The present Government has shown that wealth can be redistributed, and existing contracts broken, by the con-venient procedure of Orders in Council. The precedent should be remembered.

What a Labour Government can do depends on what, when

in opposition, it has taught its supporters to believe will be done. "Never office again without a majority" is the formula of the moment. But quality of support is as important as quantity. The Labour Party deceives itself, if it supposes that the mere achievement of a majority will enable it to carry out fundamental measures, unless it has previously created in the country the temper to stand behind it when the real struggle begins. Much of its propaganda appears to the writer—himself the least effective of propagandists—to ignore that truism. What is needed, is not merely the advocacy of particular measures of Socialist reconstruction, indispensable though that is. It is the creation of a body of men and women who, whether trade unionists or intellectuals, put Socialism first, and whose creed carries conviction, because they live in accordance with it.

The way to create it, and the way, when created, for it to set about its task, is not to prophesy smooth things; support won by such methods is a reed shaken by every wind. It is not to encourage adherents to ask what they will get from a Labour Government, as though a campaign were a picnic, all beer and sunshine. It is to ask them what they will give. It is to make them understand that the return of a Labour Government is merely the first phase of a struggle the issue of which depends on themselves. It is objected that such methods involve surrendering for a decade the prospect of office. It may be replied that, if so, impotence out of office is preferable, at any rate, to impotence in it. It does not prejudice the future, or leave a record to be lived down. But is it certain that, had the late Government spoken in that sense before coming to power, and then fallen in 1930 in the attempt to carry a measure of first-class importance, it would have been less likely to supply an alternative Government five years later?

Talk is nauseous without practice. Who will believe that the Labour Party means business as long as some of its stalwarts sit up and beg for social sugar-plums, like poodles in a drawing-room? On this matter there is at the moment a good deal of cant. The only test is the practical one; what behaviour is most conducive to getting on with the job? A distinction should be drawn, no doubt, between compliance with public conventions and conduct in matters of purely personal choice. If one is a postman, one can wear a postman's uniform, without thereby being turned into a pillar of sealing-wax. And, if Privy Councillors make up for the part, when duty requires it, by hiring official clothes from a theatrical costume-maker, who will let them for the day at not unreasonable rates, there is nothing to shed tears over, except their discomfort. The thing, all the same, though a trifle, is insincere and undignified. Livery and an independent mind go ill together. Labour has no need to imitate an etiquette. It can make its own.

It is one thing to bow down in the House of Rimmon, for practical reasons, when necessity requires it. It is quite another to press, all credulity and adoration, into the inner circle of his votaries. But the criticism on the snobbery of some pillars of the party, though just as far as it goes, does not go far enough. Those who live in glass houses should not throw stones. The truth is that, though the ways of some of the big fish are bad, those of some of the smaller fry are not much better. Five-pounders and fingerlings, we insist on rising, and—shades of Walton!—to what flies!

It will not do. To kick over an idol, you must first get off your knees. To say that snobbery is inevitable in the Labour Party, because all Englishmen are snobs, is to throw up the sponge. Either the Labour Party means to end the tyranny of money, or it does not. If it does, it must not fawn on the owners and symbols of money. If there are members of it—a small minority no doubt, but one would be too many—who angle for notice in the capitalist Press; accept, or even beg for, "honours"; are flattered by invitations from fashionable hostesses; suppose that their financial betters are endowed with intellects more dazzling and characters more sublime than those of common men; and succumb to convivial sociabilities, like Red Indians to fire-water, they have mistaken their vocation. They would be happier as footmen. It may be answered, of course, that it is sufficient to leave them to the ridicule of the world which they are so anxious to enter, and which may be trusted in time—its favourites change pretty quickly—to let them know what it thinks of them. But in the meantime, there are such places as colliery villages and cotton towns. How can followers be Ironsides if leaders are flunkies?

One cannot legislate for sycophancy; one can only expose it, and hope that one's acquaintances will expose it in oneself.

The silly business of "honours" is a different story. For Labour knighthoods and the rest of it (except when, as in the case of civil servants and municipal officers, such as mayors and town clerks, they are recognised steps in an official career) there is no excuse. Cruel boys tie tin cans to the tails of dogs; but even a mad dog does not tie a can to its own tail. Why on earth should a Labour member? He has already all the honour a man wants in the respect of his own people. He can afford to tell the tempter to take his wares to a market which will pay for them—in all conscience large enough—and himself to the devil. While the House of Lords lasts, the party must have spokesmen in it. Peerages, therefore, have very properly been undergone, as an unpleasant duty, by men who disliked them. It should in future be made clear, beyond possibility of doubt, that that reason, and no other, is the ground for accepting them. When it is necessary that a Labour peer should be made, the victim required to play the part of Jephtha's daughter should be designated by a formal vote of the parliamentary party meeting. It is not actually essential that the next annual conference should pass a resolution of sympathy with him and his wife, but it would be a graceful act for it to do so. What odious Puritanism! Yes, but the Puritans, though unpleasant people, had one trifling merit. They did the job, or, at any rate, their job. Is the Labour Party doing it?

If there is the right spirit in the movement, there will not be any question of the next Labour Government repeating the policy of office at all costs which was followed by the last. Whether it takes office without an independent majority is a matter of secondary importance compared with its conduct when it gets there. Its proper course is clear. The only sound policy for a minority Government is to act like a majority Government. It is not to attempt to enact the less controversial parts of its programme; for its opponents give nothing away, and will resist a small measure of educational reform as remorselessly as a bill for the nationalisation of the land. It is to fight on large issues, and to fight at once. It is to introduce in the first three months, while its prestige is high and its moral unimpaired, the measures of economic reconstruction which it regards as essential. It will, of course, be defeated; if it is in a minority, in the Commons, if it is in a majority in the Lords, unless its majority is such as to convince the latter that discretion is the better part of valour. In the second case, it can use the Parliament Act, supposing it to be still law, and go to the country on the abolition of the House of Lords; in the first, it must demand a dissolution. In either, it will do better for the nation and itself by forcing the issue, than by earning as its epitaph the answer which Sieyès gave to the question what he had done during the Terror: *"j'ai vécu"*; "I kept alive."

It is objected that such a policy involves sacrificing opportunities for useful work, particularly in the field of international affairs. It may—for the time being; had the late Government acted on it, Sir John Simon would have succeeded Mr. Henderson after one year, instead of after two. On a long view, however, the dilemma is less absolute than that argument suggests. The League is what the rulers of the Great Powers, and the interests behind them, permit it to be. In the light of the history of the last fourteen years, and not least of 1932–33—in the light, for example, of their attitude in the test case of Manchuria and of the tragic farce of the Disarmament Conference—can it seriously be argued that they are eager that it should itself be a power, or that even a Labour Government, if it holds office at the mercy of its opponents and the League's, can succeed, during a brief spell of precarious authority, in making it one? It is obvious that, as the world is today, no nation can save itself by itself; we must co-operate, or decline. But is it probable that international co-operation can be built on a foundation of states dominated, in their internal lives, by ideals antithetic to it? Those who cannot practise their creed under their own roof can practise it nowhere, and one contribution, at least, which a Labour Government can make to that cause is to be made at home. It is to apply to the affairs of its own country the principles which, it believes, should govern those of the world. It is to extend the area of economic life controlled by some rational conception of the common good, not by a scramble, whether of persons, classes, or nations, for individual power and profit.

Sir Arthur Salter, in contrasting the frank individualism of the nineteenth century with the improvised, half-conscious experiments in collective control of the post-war world, observes that "we have, in our present intermediate position between these two systems, lost many of the advantages of both, and failed to secure the full benefits of either." In the sphere of international, as of domestic, policy, the attempt to give a social bias to capitalism, while leaving it master of the house, appears to have failed. If capitalism is to be our future, then capitalists, who believe in it, are most likely to make it work, though at the moment they seem to have some difficulty in doing so. The Labour Party will serve the world best, not by doing half-heartedly what they do with conviction, but by clarifying its own principles and acting in accordance with them.

6

Why Britain Fights[1]

How do the mass of plain people in Great Britain view the present conflict? What thoughts stir the minds of young men when, on the threshold of their careers, they are called up for military service, and of the women who say good-bye to them? What keeps armies of workers, tenacious of their hard-won rights and not easily driven, slaving twelve hours a day to feed the all-devouring monster, and makes men complain, as it was complained lately to me, not that the pace set is too fast, but that the management is too slow? What has rallied the Trade Union and Co-operative Movements, with their millions of members, to the support of the struggle, and carried the Labour Party, with its long record of work for international goodwill, into key positions in the Government?

The British people are not ignorant of the price which war exacts. The country is full of men who fought in the last war, and who hoped that, by shouldering the burden then, they were saving others from it in the future. The first feature to catch the eye in every English village is the village war memorial, with a list of the men who went last time, and who did not come back. From 1918 to 1939 the loathing of war was unquestionably the most powerful, the most general and the most constant of political emotions. It was so powerful and so general, indeed, as to arouse some criticism among our friends abroad.

That loathing still persists. Yet once more we are fighting. We are fighting, not in spite of our hatred of war, but because

[1] Published as letter by *New York Times*, July 21, 1940.

of it. We are not fighting in obedience to the orders of our Government. Our Government is fighting in obedience to our orders. We shall continue to fight until the job is done or we are. What are we fighting for?

My countrymen are, I am afraid, an inarticulate lot. Their usual reaction to patriotic rhetoric (of which, thank heaven, there has so far not been much) is a yawn or a growl. Confronted by the question asked above, the plain man would probably begin by saying what we are not fighting for.

We are not fighting for territory; what on earth should we do with it? We expect no economic advantages; on the contrary, we know that we shall be lucky if we are not ruined. We cherish no theory of racial superiority. We have not ceased to be men because we are Englishmen, Welshmen, and Scots, and these bloodthirsty idolatries of a non-existent chosen people appear to us absurd and tedious myths, invented by hysterical professors to compensate for an inferiority complex which, but for their antics, might have passed unnoticed.

We have felt hitherto no animosity for the German people. They seem to us dangerously docile—sheep driven by any wolf. But we recognise that in economic (though not in territorial) matters they had a raw deal from the Allies in 1919, and have since had, in all matters, a rawer one from their own rulers. We realise that, if some of them are the willing tools of their tyrant, many others are his victims. We have ignored repeated breaches of solemn engagements, to the point, as our foreign friends told us, of imprudence or cowardice.

Nor, the plain man might continue, do we feel much excitement about that singularly unimperial institution called the British "Empire." The Dominions—very properly—have long been in the habit of telling us where we get off. They can secede, and know they can secede, at any moment they please, without a finger being lifted in Great Britain to stop them, which is one reason, perhaps, why they are with us in the present war. India—unless we are defeated, in which case she would presumably be partitioned between the victors—is plainly going the same way; the quicker, the better. The Irish Free State remains a neutral, with a German Minister residing tranquilly in Dublin. Not a British dog has barked.

There are scandalous enough chapters in our history; there

are still plenty of black patches which we are—too slowly— tidying up. But we see little reason to think that the steel rods and concentration camps of efficient Aryan rulers would mean a change for the better for the peoples concerned. Nor, as far as can be judged, do those peoples think so either.

Every nation is afflicted by Heaven with its own brand of fool; and, no doubt, there are a handful of British megalo- maniacs who alternately amuse and exasperate their fellow- countrymen by casting them for the role of the lords of creation. But if any one supposes that, at this time of day, the most bellicose of Cabinets—let alone Mr. Chamberlain and his troupe of tame cats—could have carried their countrymen into war to back the fancy of these Bobadils, he must be living in the moon.

What, then, are the reasons which have made this war a war, not merely of the British Government, but of the British people? They are obvious, elementary, and commonplace; but to the men in the workshops and at the front they seem, though simple, sufficient.

We are fighting, they would say, if they expressed their convictions (which, of course, they don't) to preserve a way of life which we value above life. We mean to leave it to our children, even if, in order to save it for them, we ourselves must be knocked out.

The nature and quality of that way of life can be stated in a dozen different fashions; indeed—since everyone knows it—it had best, perhaps, not be stated at all. Good faith; tolerance; respect for opinions which we do not share; loyalty to comrades; mercy to the weak; consideration for the unfor- tunate; equal justice for all—the ordinary decencies and humanities of intercourse between neighbours—these things are clearly part of it.

So is the power to speak freely one's own thoughts, to obey one's own conscience, to do one's duty as one sees it.

So is the right of the individual to be protected against violence, whether proceeding from other individuals or from public authorities; to live under a Government which he has a voice in making and unmaking; to work by all lawful means to promote the reforms and advance the causes which command his devotion, however repugnant they may be to his rulers.

So, finally, are relations between states sufficiently frank, honest and stable to permit ordinary men and women to live, work, bring up their families, and make what contribution they can to our common human heritage, without knowing that, at any moment, the ambitions of some criminal or neurotic, who has seized the controls of the frightful machinery of war, may shatter in an hour all they have spent their lives in building; obliterate their villages and towns; scatter their children in flight before merciless invaders, and leave them no choice but to submit to a soul-destroying despotism, or to lose their lives in resisting it.

We are, of course, fighting to defend our own country against horrors of that kind, and we are not ashamed of doing so. But we think that we are also defending certain simple moralities the systematic and deliberate defiance of which, as they are now defied by the Germany of Herr Hitler, makes life unendurable to men who know what freedom means. It is not for us to say whether we are right or wrong. But it is with that conviction that we are fighting, and shall continue to fight.

It would be foolish to pretend that these elementary decencies are anything like fully established in any country in any continent. Certainly, they are not in my own. But it is equally certain that, in Western Europe, we are gradually, if too slowly, conquering the citadels of economic tyranny and privilege, which remain the chief strongholds of the forces fettering the lives of common men.

What now confronts us is something at once younger and much older than the cupidities of the profit-maker, the dull egotism of property, the multitudinous injustices and hypocrisies of a capitalism which has had its day. It is a creed which holds that common men have no rights at all. It is a system which treats them, not as men, but as cattle.

No tyrant known to history has so clearly told the world the future which he is preparing for it as has the Chancellor of the German Reich. If any one doubts what that future is to be, let him read *Mein Kampf*, not in the expurgated edition prepared for Anglo-Saxon imbeciles, but in the original and authentic version. With all its ignorance and crudity, it is an impressive performance.

This evil and unhappy man is the dupe of his own wickedness. Though he advocates lies to deceive the masses, he believes, it seems, his own. If anyone replies that words are mere words, let him glance, if he can bear it, into the prison house in which the wretched German people has been tormented for six years. If anyone imagines that the machinery of physical and moral torture is reserved by the criminals concerned for slaves speaking their own language, let him study the recent story of Czechoslovakia, Poland, Norway, Denmark, Holland, Belgium, and Northern France.

I have been a soldier, though only for a short time, and, I fear, a bad one. I am not shocked overmuch by brutalities committed in hot blood under the dreadful strain of battle. The atrocities which make us feel grim are of a different order. They are not the unpremeditated barbarities of excitable and nerve-racked youths, reeling with fatigue and half frantic with fear. They are crimes committed under orders—orders drafted by baldheaded men in spectacles, sitting well out of danger, in comfortable offices a hundred miles behind the line. They are, in short, part of a deliberate and calculated system, coolly prepared and methodically applied.

In just over two years that system has been imposed by a combination of violence and treachery on seven different peoples with long and famous histories, which have enriched mankind; some eminent today in art, science, and learning; all composed of ordinary human beings like ourselves, who desired only to go about their daily work, to do their best for their children, to cultivate their own gardens, and to live at peace with their neighbours. The danger that all Europe—to mention only Europe—may succumb to it is not, therefore, remote. It is at our door.

We do not think that a world in which that system is the rule of life will be a better place. Whatever other nations may decide, we do not intend to see it. Our part is chosen and our lot is cast. Half an hour ago I said good-bye to a former student just called up for service. "What," I asked him, "are your friends saying of the report that the French have been compelled to lay down their arms?" He replied, "They are saying, 'Then it's up to us to fight all the harder.'"

We can lay no claim to any special virtue, for though we

dislike fighting, we dislike it less than the alternative. We prefer dying on our feet to living on our knees.

*   *   *

Modern war is a highly capitalised industry. To prepare for it adequately in advance involves heavy investments in plant; the diversion of manpower and resources from the arts of peace to the business of destruction; the continuous concentration of intelligence and energy on a single objective, which civilised men regard with abhorrence.

It is probably inevitable, therefore, that democracies, when reluctantly involved in the appalling task, should start it at a disadvantage, compared with those States which live in armour day and night. The former hope for the best; the latter plan the worst. The former must convince free citizens of the imminence of danger; the latter give orders and enforce them by the whip. The former await the blow; the latter choose, to suit their own designs, the time and place at which to strike.

Which attitude is least discreditable the world must judge. For good or evil, Great Britain followed the first path down to 1937, and, indeed, beyond it. If her conduct was culpable, we must all, in all parties, bear some share of the blame.

There was a general and profound hatred of war. There was a strong opposition to any policy which might involve the curtailment of expenditure designed to raise the standard of life of the mass of the population. There was a Government which, in spite of its large majority, was terrified of presenting a target to attack.

Nor, unfortunately, is that all. In the opening years of the last war the infantry sat under bombardments which the guns behind them could not answer for lack of sufficient shells. Such a miscalculation was discreditable, but it was an error that descended from the days of peace.

In the present war we have been guilty of different, but not less grave, errors, and guilty of them after the struggle had begun. For eight months we said, "Time is our ally," and then made time our enemy by wasting precious hours. We assumed that, in the matter of mobilising industry to meet the needs of war, all necessary steps were being taken with all possible speed.

We were mistaken. To attempt at this stage to assess the

responsibility of individuals would be both unjust and unwise; but the consequences remain. Whatever the reason, we failed to harness our full energies from the start. We have paid a heavy price.

That phase is now over. It vanished in one night. The debate on Norway killed it. Since then it has been buried fathoms deep, on the beach at Dunkerque and in the citadel of Calais. The former Government has disappeared, to the general relief, including those of its members whom, for political reasons, it has been thought advisable to retain. Whether in office or out of it, they no longer count.

What has replaced them is a new Government, but it is also something more. It is a new mentality, long at work beneath the surface, but now in command. The British political system permits the policy of Cabinets to drift, for considerable periods, out of touch with public opinion. But it also makes possible a sudden recovery, in which the nation teaches its rulers who is master, imposes its will, and creates, with surprising rapidity, a Government to suit itself.

It is such a recovery which we have recently witnessed. Barely four weeks have elapsed since the decisive steps were taken. To judge by the change since that date, they might be four years.

The immediate occasion for it all was a revolt in Parliament, led by the Labour Party, but supported both by the independent Liberals and a group of Tories who, to their lasting credit, put their consciences before their party. Its result is the Government headed by Mr. Churchill.

While Liberals and some Tories co-operated with admirable public spirit, it is not, I think, mere partisanship to say that the major part in the whole business was played by the Labour Party. It took the lead in the decisive debate; assumed the responsibility of refusing to serve under Mr. Chamberlain, when the latter at last realised the necessity for a reconstructed Cabinet: and rallied the Labour Movement to the support of a Government with Mr. Churchill at its head.

It now has two seats in the War Cabinet; in addition, leading members of it are in charge of three key offices, the Ministries of Supply, Labour, and Economic Warfare. Speaking broadly, it may be said that the organising of the war effort on the

military fronts is under the direction of Mr. Churchill and
those around him, and that the organising of the war effort on
the domestic and economic fronts is in the hands of Labour.
The two spheres necessarily overlap at every point, and such a
statement must not be read as implying any formal division of
responsibilities. That, or something like that, however, appears
at present to be the situation.

We must not shout till we are out of the wood, which we are
far from being. But the effects, so far, have been electrical.
The country feels that at last it has got a Government to its
mind—a Government which is single-minded in the prosecu-
tion of the war; which will tell it plainly brutal facts, however
unpleasant, and not gloss over failures; which will tolerate no
obstruction, from whatever quarter it may be threatened.

Mr. Churchill's predecessor was a master of soothing words.
Mr. Churchill states bluntly—what is obviously true—that the
events which culminated in the evacuation of Dunkerque were
"a colossal military disaster." The public, so far from being
depressed by his statement, is invigorated and inspired by it.

The Labour Movement has throughout been behind the war,
knowing only too well that, whatever else might survive a
German victory, the liberties of common men would not. But,
till recently, it was behind it rather than a responsible partner
in it. Under the late Government it supported the war—so to
say—from outside, which was all it could then do. Rightly or
wrongly, it felt grave doubts as to the sincerity of its rulers;
while they, on their side, either did not know how to put the
country on its mettle or did not dare to do so.

Possibly they underestimated the full dimensions of the job
before them; possibly they were conscious that their hold
on the public was not too secure. Whatever the reason,
they failed to demand the full measure of sacrifice which
victory requires.

One of the striking lessons of the last month is a lesson
which it should not have been necessary for experience to
teach. It is the weakness of democracy when it feels doubts as
to its leaders, and the strength of democracy when it has a
Government which it trusts. Events, of course—the disaster in
Belgium, the emergence behind the German wolf of the Italian
jackal, the *débâcle* in France—have raised the national spirit to

new heights. But the fact that the industrial population of the country, on whose efforts, not less than on those of the soldiers, victory depends, knows that leading members of the Government are men with the same experience as themselves is a priceless asset.

The Minister of Supply, Mr. Morrison, gives a catalogue of the deficiencies to be made up, and ends, "Go to it." The only comment heard is, "Thank Heaven for a man who knows his own mind and tells us what he wants!" The Minister of Labour, Mr. Bevin, has the immense task of creating the machinery by which manpower is to be organised, including a National Labour Supply Board, Area Boards, and Local Supply Committees; training centres to refit for industrial life workers previously unemployed; a national arbitration tribunal to deal with disputes which cannot be settled between employers' associations and unions; the quick transference of workers to the industries most needing them; provision for welfare and meals within factories and outside them, and a score of other urgent problems.

He tells workers they must work twelve hours a day, forgo customary holidays, and submit to restrictions on their freedom to change their jobs. Not a voice is raised in protest. The Board of Trade issues an order cutting down the consumption of goods to the value of some £250,000,000, or by roughly one-third as compared with the six months which ended November 30th last. If complaints are made, they are not vocal. Powers are conferred on the Government amounting, in effect, to *carte blanche* to nationalise any industry and property if and when the national interest so requires. In ordinary circumstances the storm raised would have been tremendous. Hardly a murmur is heard.

There is nothing very novel in war collectivism of this kind. What is striking is the rapidity with which, after a period of disastrous indecision, it is now being carried through. In addition to the heightened effort to organise swiftly for the immediate necessities of the struggle, the social equities—to use, for the sake of brevity, a deliberately vague phrase—are receiving more attention than in any previous war, and, indeed, than in some periods of peace.

Old-age pensions, the value of which had been reduced by

the rise in prices, have been substantially increased. The minimum wage of agricultural workers has been raised, not to any very glorious figure, but at any rate by something between one-quarter and one-third. Workers in the building trades have suffered much from loss of wages due to interruptions by bad weather, and have long demanded a guaranteed week. As far as government work is concerned, it has now been established. The excess profits tax has been raised to 100 per cent on profits arising after the end of March 1940; and a warning has been given by the Chancellor of the Exchequer that a sharp eye will be kept by the authorities on the expenditure of firms, to insure that the tax is not evaded or reduced by the inclusion in costs of items not essential for the purpose of the business.

The power which the Government now possesses to take over industrial concerns offers in itself a guarantee that the national cause will not be prejudiced by an undue tenderness to private interests. The trade unions are being treated as responsible partners, and are actively co-operating with the Government to speed up the production of the vast material that modern war requires.

*   *   *

In the last five years democracy has been destroyed in at least seven countries of Western Europe, exclusive, of course, of the two tyrannies themselves. It is not a conjecture, but a certainty, that if Germany is victorious, democracy will disappear from Europe altogether.

To say that the present war, while, like all major convulsions, it has many different aspects, is a war for democracy, is not, therefore, mere rhetoric, but the statement of a plain fact. That statement remains true, whatever view may be taken of the political characteristics and quality of Great Britain. She may be an unworthy champion of democracy, but she remains its champion none the less.

Those who deny that truism are merely misinformed. They do not know the realities of the European world. What, on a broad view, the change of government in Great Britain means is that a war for democracy is now being fought in a democratic spirit and by democratic methods.

The Labour Movement, in particular, finds itself confronted with a situation curiously different from that commonly anticipated in the past by most of its members. They expected that Labour would come to power after a severe, but ultimately victorious, struggle in the teeth of bitter opposition. What has actually happened is that it has been summoned by the nation to become a partner in the Government, because it was realised, in a desperate emergency, that the nation cannot be saved unless Labour assumes its full measure of responsibility.

That fact, and the results which have flowed from it, will be of profound significance in the future, if there is a future. Whether there is a future for freedom in Europe depends partly on ourselves, partly on forces outside our control. About the latter we need not concern ourselves. We can only follow such lights as we have—often, I fear, pretty dim—and do our duty as we see it. We would rather go down than live to despise ourselves. If we fight against tyranny and are defeated, we shall at least leave a memory which will nerve other men in other ages to fight with better fortune. But we shall not be defeated.

7

We Mean Freedom[1]

THE previous essays in this series have dealt with the practical application of Socialist policy to a number of topics of immediate moment. The part assigned to me is a humbler one. It is that, not of the specialist who diagnoses and prescribes for the disease, but of the attendant who induces the patient to practise the regimen ordered, by persuading him that, repulsive as at first sight it may appear, he will find it in reality, not only fortifying, but positively agreeable; that it involves the surrender of no habits or activities which a sensible man ought to wish to retain; and that, if only he will pluck up the courage to give it a trial, he will end by being astonished that he did not take to it before. I am only too conscious of my inability to utter convincingly the reassuring noises which such a role requires; but, in doing business with so experienced and wary an animal as the British lion, an approach which allays his initial alarms is undoubtedly expedient; and, not less undoubtedly, the kernel of his apprehensions is to be found in the region indicated by the title of my essay. At the suggestion that he may be bullied, manœuvred or cajoled out of what he regards as his liberty, both his interests and his idealisms at once begin to bristle; and, in my opinion, the latter, which are shared by a public to whom the former mean little, are on a long view the more formidable of the two. So I think it at once judicious and humane to attempt to soothe him at his most sensitive point.

My subject is "We Mean Freedom." No doubt, we do; but

[1] Lecture delivered for the Fabian Society in 1944, and published in *What Labour Could Do* (The Labour Book Service, 1945).

then so, in his own opinion, at least in this country, does everyone else, including the House of Lords, the Conservative Party,
the Press, the Stock Exchange, and a miscellaneous assortment
of bankers, industrialists, and landowners, all of whom cry
aloud and cut themselves with knives at the thought that the
liberties of the country may be menaced. In order to dissociate
ourselves from company so compromising, it is not sufficient
to protest our devotion to a deity which, ostensibly at least,
is also theirs. It is necessary to state what we mean by freedom,
and what is the nature of the freedom for which we stand. I
had better begin, therefore, by confessing at once that the
truth of the matter seems to me less abstruse than might be
gathered from listening to some of those who discourse on it.

There is no such thing as freedom in the abstract, divorced
from the realities of a specific time and place. Whatever else it
may or may not imply, it involves a power of choice between
alternatives—a choice which is real, not merely nominal,
between alternatives which exist in fact, not only on paper.
It means, in short, the ability to do—or refrain from doing—
definite things, at a definite moment, in definite circumstances,
or it means nothing at all. Because a man is most a man when
he thinks, wills, and acts, freedom deserves the sublime things
which poets have said about it; but, as part of the prose of
everyday life, it is quite practical and realistic. Every individual possesses certain requirements—ranging from the
material necessities of existence to the need to express himself in speech and writing, to share in the conduct of affairs
of common interest, and to worship God in his own way or
to refrain from worshipping Him—the satisfaction of which is
necessary to his welfare. Reduced to its barest essentials, his
freedom consists in the opportunity secured him, within the
limits set by nature and the enjoyment of similar opportunities
by his fellows, to take the action needed in order to ensure that
these requirements are satisfied.

It is not my intention to add yet another catalogue of
essential rights to the libraries of such lists which already
exist; but two observations apply to all of them. In the first
place, if the rights are to be an effective guarantee of freedom,
they must not be merely formal, like the right of all who can
afford it to dine at the Ritz. They must be such that, whenever

the occasion arises to exercise them, they can in fact be exercised. The rights to vote and to combine, if not wholly valueless, are obviously attenuated, when the use of the former means eviction and of the latter the sack; the right to education, if poverty arrests its use in mid-career; the right to the free choice of an occupation, if the expenses of entering a profession are prohibitive; the right to earn a living, if enforced unemployment is recurrent; the right to justice, if few men of small means can afford the cost of litigation; the right "to life, liberty, and the pursuit of happiness," if the environment is such as to ensure that, as in a not distant past, a considerable proportion of those born will die within twelve months, and that the happiness-investments of the remainder are a gambling stock.

In the second place, the rights which are essential to freedom must be such as to secure the liberties of all, not merely of a minority. Some sage has remarked that marriage would not be regarded as a national institution if, while five per cent of the population were polygamous, the majority passed their lives unsolaced and unencumbered by husbands or wives. The same is true of freedom. A society in which some groups can do much what they please, while others can do little of what they ought, may have virtues of its own; but freedom is not one of them. It is free in so far, and only in so far, as all the elements composing it are able in fact, not merely in theory, to make the most of their powers, to grow to their full stature, to do what they conceive to be their duty, and—since liberty should not be too austere—to have their fling when they feel like it. In so far as the opportunity to lead a life worthy of human beings is restricted to a minority, what is commonly described as freedom would more properly be called privilege.

As far, therefore, as matters of principle are concerned, the meaning of freedom seems to me pretty simple. The practical interpretation of principles in terms of policy and institutions is, of course, another story. Before values can become a power in everyday life, they need interests as their allies. If they prevail and win general acceptance, they do so with the limitations which those allies impose. They do not, on that account, cease to be values. The idea that they do—the description of honesty and good faith as "bourgeois morality," as though virtues ceased to be virtues when practised (if they are practised) by the middle classes, or the dismissal of political democracy with a shrug of the shoulders as "capitalist democracy," as though in a capitalist society it could be any-thing else—these and similar inanities had their run in the silly season of the 'thirties, when Bloomsbury awoke to the recon-dite fact of the existence of a class struggle and announced its discovery with blood-curdling bleats, and invitations to hunt tigers were circulated by sportsmen with whom a brave man might well have hesitated to shoot rabbits. They need no deflating, since they appear, though belatedly, to have deflated themselves. But while values remain values, even when dis-torted by interests, the perversion which they undergo at the hands of the latter is none the less serious. The conception of freedom commonly held by the well-to-do classes in England, and till recently accepted by the mass of their fellow-country-men, is a case in point.

It includes some features—tolerance, a respect for personal liberty, a belief in the virtues of representative government, an obstinate determination to hold on our own course and not to be bullied into changing our ways—which are part of the national legend, and which I, at least, admire. But the struggles by which these things were established belong to the past. In the fields where the battles of freedom are still to be won—in matters arising in the economic sphere and in the political regions closest to it—self-congratulation is less easy. As far as such issues are concerned, he must be a charitable man who does not feel that much of the eloquence devoted to applauding freedom, lamenting the menaces to it, and warning the country against surrendering its spiritual treasures for the sake of mere material benefits, is primarily directed to the preservation of the freedom at present possessed by the orators and their friends. Classes already at the top of the ladder may fall, but cannot rise. The construction which they put upon liberty is the result of that position. Whether consciously or not, it is, in large measure, a defence mechanism. Put in a nutshell, it is a doctrine of liberty which regards it as involving, not action to extend opportunities and raise individual faculty to the highest possible level, but the continued enjoyment by individuals and groups of such powers, advantages and opportunities as past history and present social arrangements may happen to have conferred upon them.

If anyone thinks such a picture is overdrawn, let him consider the positions adopted in certain current controversies. Let him study a recent report by an important association of industrialists, with its ingenuous proposal that the State should both give its blessing to the formation of combines and refrain from interfering with their freedom to manage their affairs as they think fit. Let him note the reactions of the body in whose title the words Liberty and Property are so happily united to the programmes of local authorities for the replanning of towns and acquisition of land. Let him mark the reception accorded in influential quarters to the obvious truth that, in the treatment of the controls erected during the war, the only sane course is not to scrap them indiscriminately as incompatible with economic freedom, but to distinguish between them, and, while winding up some of them as soon as circumstances allow, to recognise that there are others without the maintenance of which houses within the reach of families of small means will not be built, necessaries produced before luxuries, tonnage used in the general interest, and the consumer protected against the effects of shortages. Let him observe the successful resistance offered by the children of light in the shape of head masters to the abolition of fees in all secondary schools, on the ground that it would destroy the freedom of parents in selecting schools, though it is perfectly obvious to anyone who knows the facts that, since a large proportion of parents cannot afford the fees charged at the more expensive institutions, the freedom of all but a minority would be increased by their abolition. The premise of all these thinkers —if that word is not too violent—is the same. It is, speaking summarily, that, once emergency restrictions have been buried safely out of sight, such measure of liberty as is either possible or desirable is already secured by the existing social order; that the main menace to liberty consists in the threatened extension of the activities of public bodies into departments of economic and social life which at present escape them; and that a determined resistance to programmes of collective action is the sole safeguard, and a sufficient safeguard, for its continued preservation.

The only sound test of a political doctrine is its practical effect on the lives of human beings. The results of this doctrine we know, and it need not, therefore, be discussed at length. It is perfectly true, of course, that there have been circumstances—those, for example, of a simple economic system combined with political absolutism—in which the chief enemy of freedom was the despotism of an autocrat, and in which, therefore, the obvious way of enlarging freedom was to insist that as many spheres of life as possible should be excluded from his field of action. It should be equally obvious that, in the different conditions of an industrial civilisation, the effect of that alluring formula is precisely the opposite.

It is constantly assumed by privileged classes that, when the State refrains from intervening in any department of economic or social affairs, what remains as the result of its inaction is liberty. In reality, as far as the mass of mankind are concerned, what commonly remains is, not liberty, but tyranny. In urban communities with dense populations, or in great productive undertakings employing armies of workers, someone must make rules and see that they are kept, or life becomes impossible and the wheels do not turn. If public power does not make them, the effect is not that every individual is free to make them for himself. It is that they are made by private power—by landlords interested in increasing rents or by capitalists interested in increasing profits. The result, in either case, is not freedom, but a dictatorship, which is not the less oppressive because largely unconscious, and because those whom it profits regard it, quite sincerely, as identical with liberty.

The classical example in the past, so far as the wage-earners were concerned, was the condition of British workers in the days when trade unions were still feeble, industrial codes crude, social services in their infancy, and measures either to prevent unemployment or to enable its victims to weather the storm not yet in existence. The classical example in the present generation was the condition of many American workers down almost to yesterday. When, just over thirty years ago, I first visited Washington, I was informed on good authority that the miners in West Virginia were in trenches behind barbed wire; that the owners had a corps of snipers and a captive military balloon; and that the only individual enjoying, though precariously, a large measure of liberty, was the officer commanding the owners' troops, who was alleged—doubtless with some poetic licence—to have become a millionaire by threatening to retreat. The apparatus of coercion described long after that by a Senatorial Committee, the La Follette Committee of 1936—black lists, yellow-dog contracts, company unions, spies, undercover men, armed guards, gas-bombs, machine-guns—has since then been either demobilised or stowed safely out of sight; but why has it been demobilised? Because the Federal Government, which down to the 'thirties had no industrial policy, at last, under the brilliant leadership of President Roosevelt, acquired one; made all interference with the right of workers to combine, and the refusal to bargain collectively with them, a criminal offence; and set up administrative machinery to enforce that rule. In both countries it would be absurd to exaggerate the results which have been accomplished. In both the parent of such liberty as has been achieved is law, in the form either of trade-union regulations or of legislative enactments.

As far as Great Britain is concerned, that particular issue now seems remote. But what is true of men as producers is equally true of men as consumers. The only intellectually respectable argument against the intervention of the State in the processes of economic life consisted in the statement that the public was protected against exploitation and secured the fruits of economic progress by the mutual rivalry of producers. Each of the latter, it was held, controlled too small a proportion of the output of his industry to be able to affect the market price, which he must accept as a *datum*. Each, if a rival introduced an improvement, would be compelled to follow suit or to go out of business. Thus "greed," in the classical phrase, would be "held in check by greed," and competition would act as an automatic substitute for honesty. Whether competition ever was or can be free in the sense assumed, and whether, if it could, it would be desirable that the welfare of millions of human beings should depend—to borrow the expression of Mr. E. F. M. Durbin—on a system of conditioned reflexes, are questions which need not here be discussed. What is certain is that that state of things, if it ever existed, is today as dead as the theory which purported to be based upon it.

We do not know the extent of monopoly or quasi-monopoly in British industry. The second World War has seen no report on Trusts and Combinations such as appeared in the first. Those best acquainted with the facts refrain from divulging them. If they are in the possession of the Board of Trade, it has not seen fit to take the public into its confidence. What we know is that the movement to combination made astonishing progress in the twenty years between the wars; that as long ago as 1937 an American economist could write that British business opinion was unanimous in favouring organised action to maintain prices; that the movement has received in several industries, such as iron and steel, coal, ship-building, and cotton the encouragement of the State; that it has taken long strides forward since 1939, and that it is now openly applauded in the Press by leading British industrialists as a higher stage of industrial organisation. With the economic consequences of that situation I am not at the moment concerned; but whatever the incidental advantages of monopolistic combines, one thing is certain. It is that, since they limit the consumer's choice to goods of the quality and price supplied by the monopolist, they create semi-sovereignties which are the direct antithesis of anything that can be, or in the past has been, described as freedom. Here, again, the suggestion that capitalism, at the present stage of its history, is the guardian of any liberties but its own is an unplausible affectation. If its pre-war tendencies were to develop unchecked, it would more properly be described as the parent of a new feudalism.

The third point which I would emphasise is equally obvious. It is that, in so far as the immense aggregations of economic power characteristic of the present phase of social history threaten the liberties of men as producers and consumers, they threaten their liberties as citizens as well. Of all paradoxical creeds the most paradoxical is that of those thinkers—a diminishing, but not uninfluential band—who combine an enthusiasm for political and civil freedom with a complacent indifference to the facts, which they ignore, of economic servitude. The economic system is not merely a collection of independent undertakings, bargaining on equal terms with each other. It is also a power system. It is a hierarchy of authority; and those who can manipulate the more important levers are, directly or indirectly, consciously or unconsciously, the real rulers of their fellows.

> All ignorant, they turn an easy wheel
> Which sets sharp racks to pinch and peel.

The livelihood of men working for a small firm depends on the policy of the large firm with which it finds its market; the latter on the cartel with whose rules it must comply; and all three on decisions taken in London or New York by bland, neatly tailored gentlemen who have never seen a colliery or a cotton mill, and who, if they did, would not always know the difference between a loom and a mule or spinning-frame. A firm—to speak of the inter-war period—shuts down a plant without notice, and half a town is ruined. A combine decides on what is euphemistically called a reduction of capacity, and a whole district, like the north-east coast, is paralysed. The capital market sees money in some investment which is the fashion of the moment; coal and cotton remain unmodernised. With the assent of the City, though to the exasperation of many industrialists, sterling is over-valued; there is a miners' stoppage and what is called a general strike. For reasons which I must not now attempt to discuss, a collapse of prices sends industry over a precipice and some Governments with it. No authority exists to steady the ship before it is too late. Where the monster will next break loose, when peace returns, no one can say; but, unless he finds his master, break loose he will. The people to pay the price will be unhappy men and women trembling for their jobs.

Of all emotions the most degrading and the least compatible with freedom is fear. The brutal fact is that, as far as the mass of mankind are concerned, it was by fear, rather than by hope, that the economic system was in the past kept running—fear of unemployment, fear of losing a house, fear of losing savings, fear of being compelled to take children from school, fear of what one's wife would say when these agreeable events all happened together. If you wish to see how, before the days of full employment, the thing worked in practice, ask an employer when it was that men were easiest to drive. He will tell you that they might be awkward when times were good, but that they sweated like slaves at the very moment when a decline in trade made it uncertain whether their output would find a market, because it was then that they were frightened for their jobs. And he, poor devil, with an over-draft at his bank, was often in his heart as frightened as they were.

Whatever might be the merits of such arrangements, they were certainly incompatible with the freedom of all but the minority who profited by them, and, on any but the shortest view, with political, as well as with economic, freedom. The war should have taught us one lesson, if it has taught us nothing else. It is that it is idle to blazon Liberty, Equality, and Fraternity on the façades of public buildings, if to display the same motto in factories and mines would arouse only the cynical laughter that greets a reminder of idealisms turned sour and hopes unfulfilled. What men desire is, not paragraphs in constitutions, but results, in the form of arrangements which ensure them the essentials of a civilised existence and show a proper respect for their dignity as human beings. If they do not get them in one way, they will try to get them in another. If the interpretation given to freedom reduces it to a formal phrase, they will not fight for it against an alternative which pretends, at least, to offer them substance, not a shadow. We are not ignorant what that alternative is. Should some gentlemanly version of Fascism—it will be called, of course, not Fascism, but True Democracy—ever arrive in this country, it will be established, not by the tyranny of a ruthless minority, but as the result of the indifference of an apathetic majority, so sickened by shams as to yield to any regime which promises them the practical conditions of a tolerable life, without which freedom is a phantom.

If Socialists are to restore to the idea of freedom the magic which once belonged to it, they must bring it down to earth. They must state its meaning in realistic and constructive terms, not as a possession to be defended, but as a goal to be achieved. They must prove that it is they, not the interests that use it as a stalking-horse, who are the true champions of the faith. They must make it evident that their policy is to end economic, as well as political, tyranny, by making economic, as well as political, power responsible to authorities acting for the nation. To discuss in detail the contents of such a programme is not within my present province. Whatever else it may imply, it clearly involves, not merely—essential though that is—the wide extension of communal services needed to make available for all advantages which at present are the privilege of the few, but a genuine and decisive transference of economic sovereignty. It does not necessarily mean indiscriminate nationalisation, which is merely one method, though an important method, of achieving that result. It does mean that the key-points and strategic positions of the economic system shall be removed from the sphere of private interests and held by public bodies. It means that the State shall be equipped with the machinery needed to enable it to regulate, stimulate and direct the flow of capital into different undertakings; that the foundation services, such as banks, transport, coal and power, steel—to mention no others—shall be vested in public ownership; that monopolies shall either be treated in the same way or be strictly controlled; and that the mass of industries which continue to be carried on outside the nationalised sector shall be required to work within a framework of policy laid down by a national authority. The particular methods to be employed for effecting that transformation will be, no doubt, of great diversity, and I must not now dwell on them. The essential thing is that private interests should be subordinated to those of the majority of the nation, and that the State should be equipped with such powers and organs as may be needed to guide economic development on lines conducive to the general well-being.

Were such a policy methodically pursued, few would deny, I imagine, that the range of opportunities open to ordinary men, their control over their environment, their power of initiative in matters concerning their economic and social welfare—in short, their freedom—would be far greater than in the past it was. But it is precisely at this point, of course, in the debatable land between economics and politics, that the counter-attack is launched. I do not, I am ashamed to say—as doubtless you have discerned—study the works of economic theorists with the assiduity they deserve, for the reason—if it is a reason, and not mere weakness of the flesh—explained to her pupil by the governess in that ancient, but admirable, play, *The Importance of Being Ernest*: "Do not read Mill's chapter on the fall of the rupee, my dear; it is too exciting for a young girl." If my former much-respected colleague, Professor F. A. Hayek, who has offered in his interesting book, *The Road to Serfdom*, a recent warning against Socialism, had confined himself to a forecast of the economic catastrophes prepared by it, I cannot say that, like the devils, I should have believed and trembled, but I should certainly have trembled, even while I disbelieved. He chose as his target, however, not the economics of Socialism, but the political nemesis which, he is convinced, it entails. And here, perhaps, one of the prospective serfs will not be thought presumptuous if he hazards an opinion on the destiny awaiting him.

The villain in Professor Hayek's tragedy is, of course, Planning; and Planning he defines as the "central direction of all economic activity according to a single plan, laying down how the resources of society shall be 'consciously directed' to serve particular ends in a particular way." This demon, once out of his bottle, reveals criminal potentialities which seem almost illimitable. His career begins with the discovery that no society and no assembly can conceivably agree on any major matter of economic policy. He next proceeds to remedy this unfortunate defect of democratic institutions by appointing himself and his fellow-demons as dictators. Once firmly in the saddle, he substitutes administrative decrees for the rule of law, and uses them to abolish both the workers' choice of occupations and the consumers' choice of goods. Having conquered the economic sphere, he launches a campaign against the realm of the spirit, where freedom might be expected to make its last stand. He employs violence and deceit—the concentration camp and the Press—to secure the appearance of an illusory unanimity. The curtain falls on a world in which tolerance, freedom of thought and speech, personal liberty, objective science, private and public morality, have alike been extinguished. Universal darkness covers all.

Professor Hayek's book has been composed with genuine emotion and a sincerity which commands respect. He writes, as Burke was said to speak, with the expression of a man confronted by assassins. His honesty and competence are both beyond question, and I have no wish to treat his warnings lightly. His history—his account, for example, of German influences on British social thought and of the causes of the British movement to monopoly—is not always, in my judgment, according to light; nor does experience seem to me to confirm the view, which I understand him to hold, that the major issues of economic policy are of their nature such that a democracy, when faced by them, is incapable of reaching sufficient agreement to permit of action. These points, however, are merely the out-works of his argument; and, even were they abandoned, its citadel would still stand. Let me, before reconnoitring it, present him with an admission. Human institutions are merely instruments. All of them—law-courts and police, armies and navies, churches and schools—can be, and have been, used for bad ends. It is perfectly true that public control over the processes of economic life can be used in the same way. It is perfectly true, again, that authority armed with coercive power has often been, and in some countries still is, the enemy of freedom. But to make much of these points is, it seems to me, to labour truisms. The question which matters is not whether, as everyone admits, the abuses feared *may* in certain circumstances occur. It is whether they must necessarily occur, whatever the circumstances and whatever the precautions taken against them—or, at any rate, whether the probability of their occurrence is so great that the only prudent course is to acquiesce in the continuance of existing evils, in order to avoid the more appalling *débâcle* foretold by Professor von Hayek. If my answer to that question differs from his, the principal reason is, I suppose, that I disagree with him on two points. I do not accept his conception of planning, and I do not accept his view of the State.

On the first point, having no pretensions to speak as an economist, I touch with diffidence. Planning, like Capitalism or Socialism, is obviously a genus with several different species. Professor Hayek appears to me to identify it with one species and one alone, and that, to my mind, the least attractive member of the family. He means by it, if I understand him rightly, a comprehensive programme, embracing the whole range of economic activities, under which the quantity and quality of all articles to be produced, from steel plants to pins, and the occupation and payment of every individual, are prescribed in advance for a term of years by a central authority—an authority uninfluenced by the views of consumers and producers, acknowledging no responsibility, however indirect, to a representative assembly, and conducting its affairs by the issue of orders the infringement of which is a criminal offence. Given those assumptions, it is not surprising that a totalitarian monster should emerge as his conclusion, for the author has been at pains to include totalitarianism among his premises. Whether, and in what degree, such a picture of planning corresponds with the Russian or German varieties, I have not the knowledge to say. The version of planning suggested by Professor von Hayek is, doubtless, a possible one, and his readers should be grateful to him for developing its implications. To imply, however, as he appears to do, that the procedure whose horrifying consequences he portrays with such force alone needs to be considered, or that all other procedures must necessarily lead to the same fatal goal, is to beg all questions. It is as fanciful as to dismiss parliamentary institutions as futile on the strength of their futility in certain countries which have tried them, or to suggest that a public system of education—itself an example of planning on a large scale—is necessarily corrupting, because some states have employed it as an engine of corruption.

Planning, like parliaments and public education, is not a simple category. Its results depend, not on the label attached to it, but on the purposes which it is designed to serve, the methods which it employs in order to realise them, and the spirit which determines the choice of both. If, for example, the essential characteristic of a planned economy be regarded as consisting, not as Professor Hayek seems to suggest, in a detailed budget of production, but in the transference of responsiblity for the higher ranges of economic strategy from profit-making entrepreneurs to a national authority, his mystery of iniquity is attenuated to a mare's-nest, and his bloodthirsty Leviathan becomes a serviceable drudge.

On that more modest view, it is not necessary that a single central body should intervene in every corner of economic life; it is enough that the sector controlled by it should be sufficiently important to enable the State to take or to determine the major decisions on matters such as investment, credit policy and employment, on which the general welfare depends. It is not necessary that it should plan every detail of production; it is sufficient that it should issue to the public utility corporations, or other productive units responsible to it, instructions as to the general policy which they are to pursue—for example, with regard to output, costs, prices, and the erection of new plants—and that they should conduct their operations within that framework, which itself, of course, would be made after consultation with them and would be subject to public criticism. It is not necessary that it should conscribe workers, assign them their occupations, and dictate their movements; it can leave those concerned to engage them in the ordinary way, by the offer of such inducements as are needed to attract them. It would not have the same motives as the private monopolist for maintaining prices at a level higher than that needed to cover costs, and it might find it convenient in particular cases—for example, on grounds of health—to sell at a loss; but the consumer would remain as free as he is today to suit his own tastes. It could hardly acquiesce in a group of workers in a strong strategic position forcing an advance at the expense of their fellows merely in virtue of their bargaining power; and the Trade Union Movement would have to decide whether, in refusing to exploit to the full that particular advantage of capitalism, it lost more than it gained. Apart from that case, it is not easy to specify what, if any, economic freedoms would disappear as a result of the substitution of a public authority, pursuing a deliberate production and investment policy, for a group of large private combines or a welter of small firms. In so far as economic freedom depends on the removal of the fear of unemployment, fair standards of remuneration, opportunities of promotion uninfluenced by pull and favouritism, the abolition of private monopoly and the contraction of the area of life where the battle is to the strong, it seems reasonable to say that it would be substantially increased.

The conventional retort to such a statement—I do not suggest that it is Professor von Hayek's—is to charge those who make it with a sordid materialism. The serfs, it is said, might be less uncomfortable; but their gains in one sphere would be more than counterbalanced by their losses in another. As cogs in the impersonal mechanism of an authoritarian state, they would have bartered their dignity as citizens and men—their initiative, their responsibility, their right to lead their own lives and make a mess of them if they pleased—for a shot of morphia in the soul.

It is obvious that, if a despotic Government enlarges its control over economic affairs, it will use the only methods which it understands, and manage them as a despot. But why assume despotism? It is as possible to plan for freedom as for tyranny. The idea that there is an entity called "the State," which possesses, in virtue of its title, uniform characteristics existing independently of the varying histories, economic environments, constitutional arrangements, legal systems, and social psychologies of particular states, and that these characteristics necessarily combine the manners of a Japanese customs officer with the morals of a human tiger, is a pure superstition. It is a piece of mysticism, which is pardonable in persons brought up on their knees before some mortal god, but which is none the less a bluff. Half a century ago, when we were informed by philosophers fed on Hegel that the State represented our higher selves, it was an optimistic bluff. Today, when we are sometimes told that the State is the product of one of the nastier Freudian complexes, it is liable to be a pessimistic bluff. But it is a bluff in either case.

The State is an important instrument; hence the struggle to control it. But it is an instrument, and nothing more. Fools will use it, when they can, for foolish ends, and criminals for criminal ends. Sensible and decent men will use it for ends which are decent and sensible, and will know how to keep fools and criminals in their place. What exactly, moreover, does the State in this connection include? Are the Metropolitan Water Board and the London Passenger Board part of it? Is it suggested that public liberties were imperilled when the former succeeded the eight water companies which preceded it, and the latter introduced a measure of unity into the passenger service, and both were made responsible to the appropriate departments? If not, why should they be threatened merely because a group of banking, transport, colliery, power, and steel undertakings go the same way, or because all of them are required to account for their proceedings to a central authority, with power to issue instructions as to the policy they shall pursue?

The truth is that, in the matter of civil and political liberties, the real issue lies, at any rate in this country, on a different plane from that where some prophets of the coming slavery are disposed to seek it. The former depend principally on freedom of speech and writing; freedom of worship; freedom of meeting; freedom in the choice of occupations; and freedom to combine. The latter depend partly on the former, partly on the existence of constitutional arrangements for the maintenance of representative and responsible government. The sole security for the preservation of either is a public opinion which is determined to preserve them. There is no reason whatever why that security should be weakened merely because certain industries are owned and administered by public bodies, and those bodies are guided in their procedure by instructions from a further body, which can take a more comprehensive view of the national needs than is practicable for any one of them. On the contrary, given such an arrangement, it would be both possible and desirable for the ability of the citizen to make his wishes known and his criticisms felt to be a good deal more effective than it commonly is today. When industries are nationalised, there is much to be said for attaching to each a council representative of the principal groups of consumers using their output, with powers of investigation, criticism, and publicity from which private monopolists are at present immune. Associations of producers would naturally be represented on the bodies directing different services, and would add to their present protective functions that of consultants and advisers as to the staffing of works and improvements of productive processes. Regular reports would dispel the atmosphere of artificial darkness in which a good many economic matters, which ought to be common knowledge, are at present shrouded.

The truth is, of course, that the transference of property to public hands is a means, not an end. Its success depends, not on the mere change of ownership, which, though the first step, is no more, but on the degree to which advantage is taken of the opportunity offered by it to carry through measures of reorganisation which private enterprise was unable or unwilling to undertake, to enlist the active co-operation of employees, and to secure first-class management. Such reforms require time. Criticism on the initial phases of a process which must necessarily be lengthy is, therefore, to be welcomed. The essential point is that a Government should not, in nationalising an industry, regard the first step as the last, but should have a clear conception of the subsequent stages. Its aim should be, not merely to keep the undertakings concerned rubbing along rather better than under private ownership, but to make them a model on which the workers in them look with pride, those in other industries with admiration and envy, and the public with confidence. In some cases, such as coal-mining, it should take steps to reconstruct, not only economic organisation, but the social environment as well. In all it must attempt to create a new *moral* by devolving increased responsibilities on the workers, even if at first they are reluctant to assume them, and must ensure that experiments with that end in view are pressed steadily forward. Nor must it forget the necessity for improving management standards. Thirty years ago, Lord Haldane argued that the human qualifications required by managers were not less important than the technical, and urged, in connection with the coal industry, the establishment of a staff college to cultivate the necessary *esprit de corps*, initiative, and capacity for leadership. His proposals have wider applications than those contemplated by him. A Socialist Government might do worse than explore them.

As far, therefore, as mere questions of machinery are concerned, anticipations of the eclipse of political and civil liberty by any form of Socialism probable in this country seem to me to contain more emotion than reason. The serious danger is the opposite. It is not that democracy may be sacrificed to the reckless pursuit of economic freedom. It is that the establishment of the conditions of such freedom may be too long delayed, and that the failure to achieve it may discredit democracy. Socialists ought to recognise the reality of that danger, and plan their strategy to anticipate it. Economic freedom involves a transference of the authority required in order to plan and direct certain major economic activities from the agents of property-owners to organs acting on behalf of the nation and responsible to it. In an industrial society it can be achieved in that way, and it can be achieved in no other. Hence, while I am not lacking, I hope, in enthusiasm for the further development of the communal side of Socialism, I regard it, in the present juncture, except in so far as it is concerned with education and health, as secondary to the conquest of economic power.

It is of the first importance, in my opinion, that the next Labour Government should not devote its whole energies to measures of amelioration—though some of them are essential—but should make it its central objective to bring the key-points of the economic system under public control; should have its measures for attacking that objective prepared in advance, as, doubtless, they have been; should introduce them at once, in the first months of taking office, while its prestige is still high; and should stand to its guns, to the point, if necessary, of a dissolution. What matters is not that the party should advance a glittering programme, with promises for everyone, but that it should put the nation on its mettle. It is that it should concentrate on a limited number of essentials, should tell the public frankly why it holds them to be indispensable, and should prove the sincerity of its convictions by showing that, rather than abandon them, it is willing to lose office. If it is defeated, it will temporarily be deprived of power; but it will later recover it, with authority, when it does so, to act on its programme. If, as in 1929–31, it defeats itself by sacrificing its principles in order to remain in office, it not only exposes itself to endless blackmail, but destroys both the *moral* of its supporters and the confidence of the general public, in the absence of which a Labour Government has hardly more power in office than out of it. Nor ought we to forget that, in the present state of the world, it is not merely the future of one country which is at stake. If we in Great Britain can show that it is possible to carry forward into the economic jungle the frontiers of government by consent, responsible administration, and the supremacy of general over particular interests, other peoples, in their varying ways, will follow the same road. If we cannot, we leave a free hand to whatever creed other than Socialism may be waiting to seize the vacant throne; and creeds do not die merely of military defeat. But I believe that, if we mean business, we can do the job.

8

Beatrice Webb, 1858–1943[1]

THE death of Mrs. Webb on April 30, 1943, deprived the
Academy of a distinguished member, whose contributions
to the worlds of thought and of affairs remain of permanent importance. For over half a century she had laboured
in both with single-minded devotion. At once student and
reformer, historian, economist, and pamphleteer, an experienced observer of politics and the joint author of books which
opened a new chapter in English sociology, she drove, without
flagging or losing sight of her goal, several horses abreast, and
her achievements are too diverse to be easily summarised.
When asked her profession, she modestly described herself as a
social investigator; but her mastery of her own specialisms had
not narrowed her range or atrophied her emotions, and her
friends knew her at moments when she spoke as a seer. The
significance of her work and her husband's—one cannot think
of them apart—will be more justly estimated half a century
hence than it can be today.

I

Beatrice Potter was born in 1858, the youngest but one of
nine daughters. With grandparents floated to fortune from
farm and weaver's cottage when cotton became king, and then
via radical politics into the reformed House of Commons, she
knew the rise of the Great Industry and its political sequel, not
as a story in books, but as a chapter in her family history. She

[1] Reprinted, by permission, from the *Proceedings* of the British Academy, Vol.
XXIX.

could gossip with Bright in his old age, as the descendant of a
supporter who had stood by his side in the great days of the
League; stayed, on her first visit to Lancashire, with relations
who had remained operatives on the Rossendale moors: and
was not tempted to exaggerate the immutability of economic
systems or to be unduly impressed by the capricious favours they
confer. The career of her father underlined the same lesson. He
had intended to lead the life of a country gentleman; but a
turn of the wheel, which was not a misfortune for the budding
sociologist, sent him also into affairs. When the financial crisis
of 1847–48 carried off his modest fortune, school and family
connections secured him a partnership in a firm of timber
merchants at Gloucester and a directorship of the Great
Western Railway. Other directorships followed, including the
presidency of the Grand Trunk Railway of Canada, together
with a mass of miscellaneous undertakings of a kind which
today would be epitomised as Big Business. His special gift, if
his daughter may be trusted, was not for the tactical routine,
but for planning and negotiation. Readers of *My Apprenticeship*
will recognise with amusement in the portrait of him there
drawn some traits which remind them of her formidable
persuasiveness.

Richard Potter was not the slave of his success, nor was he of
the magnates who treated business as a mystery. His daughters,
with whom he discussed his affairs freely, made the acquaintance of the associates in different enterprises whom he invited
to his house, and also—for he was a cultivated man with a wide
circle of friends—of persons eminent in science and letters. The
juvenile Miss Potter pursued self-culture with the remorseless
intensity of youth, translating *Faust* at fifteen, and attacking
next year the rocky fastnesses of Jewish history and English
law; but the earlier passages in her diary leave the impression
that her education owed less to governesses and to a year at a
fashionable school than to the ceaseless debate on books,
scientific and philosophical theories, and problems of religion
and politics which she heard about her as she grew up. The
death of her mother, a remarkable woman, whose diversity of
attainments was the subject of admiring comment by Taine,
closed six years divided between Mr. Potter's country houses
in Gloucestershire, Westmorland, and Wales, London seasons—

"riding, dancing, flirting and dressing-up"—and occasional long tours in Italy and Germany. Beatrice became at twenty-four the head of her father's household, administered his considerable income, acted as his secretary and counsellor, and acquired a sufficient acquaintance with the ramifications of his interests to cause him to suggest that she should be given a formal status as his business associate. She used later to ascribe part of her skill in marshalling and analysing the data of her inquiries to the apprenticeship served when she grappled with his affairs.

If increased responsibilities were a useful discipline for a future career, they did not make easier the choice of one. Her diary during these years shows her finding her way to the religious position which she was to hold throughout her life, but distracted to the point of misery by uncertainty how best to use her powers. Since womanhood she had found society, with its "occupational disease of vanity," increasingly distasteful, and had hoped to devote herself to intellectual work. But was she capable of serious work? And, if so, in what field? Her sympathies were keen; but her mind, as well as her emotions, required to be satisfied. In childhood and adolescence she had owed much to Spencer, her parents' most intimate friend. At twenty-five she had outgrown him. The sage, whose long suit was not humour, pressed her, with kindly obtuseness, to investigate "the absorbent organs in the leaves, roots and seeds of plants." She knew that the theme on which her heart was set was the strange ways of man in commerce with his kind, and that the study of that subject demanded methods of its own, on which the famous analogy between animal and social organisms threw but doubtful light. To observe poverty at first hand she undertook the management of a block of working-class dwellings, and did a spell of visiting for the Charity Organisation Society, then at the height of its reputation. She found the experience too exclusively pathological to be other than misleading. With few guides to help her, she seemed condemned to endless groping. Yet she knew what she wanted. "If I were a man and had an intellect, I would leave political action and political theorising to those with faith, and . . . try to describe accurately and proportionately what actually happened in the different strata of society, more especially the spontaneous

growth of organisation—try and discover the laws governing
its birth, life, and death."

The circle was broken, less by an effort of the intellect, than
by what she came to call her "sentimental journey." It
occurred to her to make the acquaintance of her mill-working
relations, and, through them, of a region of industrial England
which, in spite of her family connections with it, was still
unknown to her. In the guise of Miss Jones, the daughter of a
Welsh farmer bent on seeing the life of a Lancashire manufacturing town, she paid her cousins at Bacup the first of
several visits, lived in a weaver's cottage as one of the family,
and was introduced to their friends. The experience came to
her as a revelation. She saw from the inside, what in London
she had missed, the normal life of a working-class community.
The simplicity, unworldliness, and religious faith of her
friends—"a page of Puritan history"—profoundly stirred her
feelings. The intellectual stimulus was equally keen. It was
men and women like her hosts, overworked, underfed, and
under-educated, who had covered the north with Noncon-
formist chapels, planted a Co-operative store in every village,
and created, in the Lancashire cotton unions, the most powerful and best disciplined labour organisations that the world had
yet seen. To study society, not only through documents and
books, but by personal contact with human beings, had been
her ambition. She returned to London convinced that it was
her vocation. "I had decided to become an investigator of
social institutions."

To act on the decision required leisure. It demanded also
concentration on a specific field of work. The enforced withdrawal from social obligations caused by the sudden illness of
her father, to whom she was deeply attached, in the autumn of
1885, gave her time to clarify her ideas as to methods of social
study. Reading and reflection strengthened her conviction that,
in order to be fruitful, it must rest on a broader foundation of
carefully sifted evidence than had commonly been thought
necessary. The two essays written in 1886 on *The Rise and
Growth of English Economics* and *The Economic Theory of Karl
Marx*, brief extracts from which were later included in *My
Apprenticeship*, show the way her mind was moving. They were
her salute and farewell to deductive economics.

The importance of continuous research into the facts of social organization was not in the later eighties the commonplace which it has since become. The sympathies of the circles in which Miss Potter moved were periodically stirred by reports of the existence of an underworld of misery; but the truth that emotion is impotent without knowledge had made few converts in high places. Full and accurate knowledge of social conditions was not, indeed, too easy to obtain. The provision of official information has usually developed as a by-product of the extension of official activities. The sources supplying it, invaluable as far as they went, were in the eighties both scantier and more selective than those available today. Nor, in spite of half a century of work by statistical societies—some of it of high quality—had private enterprise yet done much to fill the gap. English economic speculation had a distinguished history, but rigour in verifying its hypotheses had not been its longest suit. The first great inquiry into urban life and work, the parent of a long line of subsequent studies, though projected, was not yet launched. Funds for research into social and industrial conditions were not easily unlocked. "In London," the authors of *Industrial Democracy* could write in 1897, "the wealthiest of all cities in the world, and the best of all fields of sociological investigation, the sum total of all endowments for this purpose does not exceed £100 a year."

In such circumstances social investigation, in any systematic form, had the difficulties, as well as the charms, of a pioneering venture. Miss Potter continued to spend the greater part of each year with her father till his death in January 1892; but, once a rearrangement of his affairs had lightened her duties, she felt the need of a limited objective, and the question which perplexed her was what target to select. The answer was supplied by her cousin by marriage, Charles Booth. Dissatisfied, like her, with generalisations based on "a series of assumptions very imperfectly connected with the observed facts of life," he was planning his inquiry into *The Life and Labour of the People of London*. He invited her to collaborate in it. She started work on the part assigned to her, a study of Dock Labour in the Tower Hamlets, in March 1887; and went on to investigate the scandals in the manufacture of cheap clothing in East London loosely summarized as sweating. The association with

Booth was a landmark in her development. Her final position was not his, but her work for him brought her more than a modest reputation for reliable research. It taught her to try her conclusions by quantitative tests, and, without blunting the edge of her ardour, gave it a realistic toughness which both the undisciplined ally and the opponent not at home with his brief sometimes found disconcerting. Five years later, when her contributions to Booth's survey had been followed by her first book, *The Co-operative Movement in Great Britain*, and the study of Trade Unionism was already on the stocks, a more important turning-point was reached. In the summer of 1892 she married Sidney Webb.

II

Mrs. Webb's decision to devote her life to sociological research had been prompted by a belief in knowledge as the key to a better world. Her intellectual conscience was exacting and she accepted the obligations which that belief imposes. Apart from her faith in science, she did not start with a creed. Her objection to "these gigantic experiments, State education and State intervention in other matters," had been confided to her diary in 1884. "Political agnosticism, tempered, by individualist economics," remained her statement of her position when, some three years later, she began assisting Booth. Her conversion to Socialism, which had taken place, in all but name, by the time she had completed her book on Co-operation, was the result, not the cause, of her work as an investigator. Though she joined the Fabian Society in 1893—not without some qualms, which proved needless, lest political associations should impair her intellectual detachment—more than a decade elapsed before she played an active part in it. As her influence grew, she used it to promote particular reforms of whose importance she was convinced; but she thought that her primary duty in life was that of a scholar, not of a propagandist. It was to reveal by her work the possibilities contained in the application of scientific methods to the study of society.

Except for the claims of public duties, which at times were heavy, and for eighteen months spent on visits to the United States and the Dominions, the Far East, and Russia, she practised her craft for approximately half a century. The twenty odd volumes in which, almost always as joint author with her husband, she was concerned during that period fall into five main groups. They include four books on working-class organization and history; ten volumes on English Local Government; three substantial works and various shorter pieces on the reform of the Poor Laws; two books specifically devoted to Socialism; and a group of miscellaneous writings, of which the most striking are *My Apprenticeship*—the least egotistical of autobiographies, which characteristically turned into a social history—and the elaborate study of Soviet Communism.

Not all of these works stand on the same level. Like those of most writers who have been active over a long period, the books of the Webbs reflect different phases in their authors' lives and thought. Some, like *The History of Trade Unionism* and *English Local Government*, the latter of which appeared at intervals over a period of nearly thirty years, were the result of prolonged investigations in fields which had previously been little explored. Others were written quickly, and dealt with topics of current discussion. The common characteristic, which sets its stamp on all of them, is a matter less of style than of substance. It is the impression conveyed of large reserves of ordered knowledge. Whatever the subject, it is handled with respect. Whether the result is a brochure, like that on *English Teachers and their Professional Organisations* or a volume on the scale of *The Parish and the County*, there is the same patient care in assembling the materials, and the same self-restraint in refraining from generalisation till the evidence has been sifted. Even those of their books which were designedly written to appeal to a wide public are marked by a range of information and a maturity of thought which sets them in a class apart from other *pièces de circonstance*. The conclusions advanced in them may be summarily expressed, but they have not been reached in haste. If the object of their authors is to persuade, as well as to inform, it is persuasion by an appeal, not to ignorance, but to knowledge.

"The 'Webb speciality'," they wrote, in explaining their procedure, "has been a study, at once historical and analytic, of the life-history of particular forms of social organisation during the last three or four centuries, such as the Trade Union and

Co-operative Movements in the United Kingdom and English
Local Government. . . . The task before us was to discover . . .
the recurrent uniformities in constitution and activities showing
the main lines of development, together with all the varieties
of structure and function arising in particular places, in
particular decades, or within peculiar social environments."
Both authors believed in planning, and the industry which
they planned first was their own. They were assisted by
secretaries—their one extravagance—to whom they gave an
invaluable training in research; but they did not spare themselves. The materials required for their historical works
were widely dispersed. The authors, who had started their
honeymoon with a visit to Dublin to examine the records of
Irish trade societies, spent part of each summer on voyages
of exploration. For the books on Trade Unionism they not
only used the wealth of sources available in London, but
ransacked the archives of all important unions in the provinces,
and of the great majority of smaller ones. The sources for
the study of Local Government were more voluminous. In
the process of discovering and making extracts from parish,
county, manorial and borough records, they visited, singly or
together, some hundreds of villages and towns, from Cornwall
to Northumberland and from Neath to Norwich. They did not
rely only on documents, but made a point of seeing in action
the organisations concerned, by attending in person the
meetings of trade unions, trades councils, and local government bodies. Nor did they confine themselves to the information
to be obtained by watching institutions at work. An interviewer
at once charming and inexorable, with a unique gift for making
the dumb speak and the loquacious talk to the point, Mrs.
Webb had discovered, when she worked for Booth, the lessons
to be learned from conversations with a purpose. In the course
of her inquiries into dock labour and the clothing trade, she
had put through their paces a long list of workers, employers,
factory and sanitary inspectors, school board officers, and
representatives of philanthropic agencies; and finally, to see
how a sweated industry looks from the inside, had taken lessons
in tailoring and obtained employment in a succession of
workshops as a "plain trouser hand." She did not forget the
value of oral evidence, or the art of eliciting it, when the time

came for their more massive works. The "method of the interview" contributed not a little to the realism of the Webbs' interpretations. They gave it a place, side by side with more formal resources, in the repertory of the investigator. To watch a witness undergoing their skilful third degree was sometimes amusing.

The subjects on which the Webbs wrote were suggested by the problems of their day; but the authors took no short cuts. They planned their major works on the principle that, in the study of society, the longest way round is often, not merely the shortest, but the only way, home. Their field of investigation once determined, they resisted the temptation—long the economist's foible—to find formulae of general application, and attacked specific problems piecemeal, seeking solutions which could be tested by an appeal to facts. Of the generalisations suggested by them some, doubtless, will be modified or rejected; others have yielded fruit as well as light. If discovery is the revelation of significant, but previously unrealised, relations between phenomena, then in their own sphere they were discoverers.

The researches of Miss Potter, as she then was, into Sweating and Co-operation, which turned upside down widely accepted ideas, are early cases in point. They are described at some length in *My Apprenticeship*, and need not here be more than mentioned. As the result of her work on the former, the picturesque myth of an endless chain of sub-contractors, with a parasitic Jewish middleman as the villain of the piece, went the way of other legends. Henceforward, it was evident, the problem was, not the removal of exceptional scandals, but the maintenance, by voluntary combinations and legislative enactments, of proper standards of employment over the whole field of industry. Her ability to see facts through plain glass, and to cause others to do the same, was equally conspicuous in her study of the Co-operative Movement. Co-operation—to a generation conscious of tightening social strains a word of reassurance—had been widely interpreted to mean the multiplication of societies of producers dividing profits among all participants in the business. Miss Potter showed that, except here and there, the British version of Co-operation meant nothing of the kind. Economic democracy, as practised by the great majority of co-operators, implied neither self-governing workshops, nor profit-sharing with employers. It involved the supply of goods, and wherever possible their production, for the service of consumers by agents appointed by them; the payment of a fixed rate of interest on capital; and the elimination of profit by the return to the purchaser of any surplus arising between prices and costs.

Miss Potter's conclusions did not pass uncriticised; but they had the facts on their side, and are today a commonplace. *The Co-operative Movement in Great Britain* was widely translated, and its influence on co-operative policy was not confined to this country. Its importance to its authoress was that of a starting-point. In answering one question, it suggested two more. If the essence of Co-operation was the sovereignty of the consumer, what role was to be assigned to the vocational organisations of wage-earners, whose struggles, at the moment when she was writing, were more in the public eye than the almost unnoticed expansion of Retail Stores and Wholesales? If the natural units for the discharge of certain economic functions were associations of purchasers, might there not also be a wide range of services which could more appropriately be entrusted to public authorities? The views of Mrs. Webb and her husband on the second question were stated in several of their subsequent works. The first, which had occurred to her while she was still at work on Co-operation, was the occasion of their researches into Trade Unionism. It is a comment on the charge of bureaucratic propensities sometimes brought against the Webbs that the six years following their marriage should have been devoted to the study of voluntary organisations.

On the appearance of *Industrial Democracy* a reviewer expressed surprise that writers so gifted should have wasted their talents in investigating institutions so unimportant as Trade Unions. If the world of organised labour is no longer today the misty region which it was when the Webbs first turned their searchlight on it, it is partly to their efforts that the change is due. Trade Unionism, throughout its history, has had a dual character. It has been at once a body of professional associations, and a social movement focusing the aspirations of different groups of wage-earners and reflecting their reactions to the ebb and

flow of politics and ideas. The relative importance of these
different aspects has varied at different times; but in England,
unlike some other countries, neither has completely over-
shadowed the other. *The History of Trade Unionism*, which no
subsequent work has yet superseded, does justice to both. It
throws its high lights on the slow welding of scattered clubs of
journeymen into national organisations; the long struggle for
the right of professional association; the development of
industrial policies appropriate to the varying circumstances of
different trades; and the changing relations between Trade
Unionism and the State. The authors had few secondary works
to help them—they had to compile their own census of trade
unionists, which figures later published by the Board of Trade
confirmed—but the influence exercised by their book was due
as much to the spirit in which it was written as to the addition
which it made to knowledge. Studiously unemotional in tone,
commanding respect by its scholarship, and candid, when
evidence gave out, in admitting ignorance, it lowered feverish
temperatures and turned on sensationalism a cooling stream of
facts. Trade Unions, it appeared, were not an appropriate
theme for impassioned denunciation or undiscriminating
eulogy. They were prosaic institutions, which, like other
institutions, had their virtues and their defects, but which, if
submitted to dispassionate study, had some lessons to teach
that the economist, the political scientist, and even the statesman, might do well to ponder.

The History of Trade Unionism was the first instalment of the
Webbs' work on the subject; but it was only the first. The
question of the economic effects of trade unions raised more
controversial issues, which were discussed at length in *Industrial
Democracy*. By the nineties the denunciation of Trade Unionism
as "contrary to the principles of political economy" was,
except in odd corners, a thing of the past; but a faint flavour
of economic impropriety still continued to cling to it. Its
purpose was admittedly to maintain minimum standards
of wages and working conditions which no employer, however
hard-pressed, could evade. Was there truth in the allegation
that the pursuit of that objective must necessarily be prejudicial
to economic progress?

In demolishing what little remained of the theoretical basis of the earlier attacks on Trade Unionism the authors had an easy task. Their analysis of the effects of prescribing minimum standards of employment, which was the kernel of their argument, broke what was then new ground. The most general and characteristic of Trade Union policies was the common rule; and the common rule, so far from being incompatible with economic efficiency, was actually conducive to it. It encouraged the selection for employment of the most competent workmen; stimulated management to discover methods of reducing costs by the progressive improvement of machinery and organisation; and promoted the most effective utilisation of the nation's resources by compelling trades which were parasitic, in the sense of using up the energies of successive relays of workers under conditions incompatible with health and vigour, either to mend their ways or to go out of existence. If the argument was valid, the conclusions implicit in it, though suggested by a study of the effects of Trade Unionism, had obviously a more general application. The legal enforcement of minimum standards of safety and sanitation had been the object of a long series of Factory and Public Health Acts. Why should a similar enforcement of minimum standards of remuneration be regarded as a heresy which must provoke an economic nemesis? *Industrial Democracy* was the first book to argue convincingly and at length the case for the policy later embodied in the Trade Boards Acts of 1909 and 1918. The forecasts which the authors permitted themselves in their concluding chapter, if they overestimated, like most prophecies, the pace of development, did not err greatly as to its direction. The future, they suggested, would see, not, as some theorists of the left then supposed, the supersession of combinations of wage-earners by the action of a paternal State, but a modification of their functions. It lay with a Trade Unionism relying, for the advancement of the wage-earner's standard of life, on legislation, not less than on collective bargaining; extending government by consent from the political into the economic sphere; and increasingly becoming, as the area of public enterprise widened, an expert adviser whose counsel was sought on all matters relating to the welfare and professional competence of different bodies of producers.

"We may distinguish, as the dominant note of the last

three-quarters of a century, an ever-growing elaboration of
organised common action. What was formerly left to the
individual household to provide, or left altogether unprovided,
is now, to an ever-increasing extent, provided for large numbers of households by some collective administration. . . .
Without the common rule that the law lays down and without
the services that the municipality supplies, the citizen of the
twentieth century would usually find it impossible to live." It
was this "spontaneous undergrowth of social tissue," rather
than the more dramatic aspects of political action, on which,
throughout their lives, the Webbs' interest was focused. Partly
for that reason, partly because their study of working-class
movements had convinced them that the lessons derived from
voluntary associations required to be supplemented by a
study of the compulsory organisations in which men were
grouped as citizens, their researches took a new turn.

The two preceding decades had seen the modernisation of
county government, and an impressive expansion of municipal
enterprise. The emergence of the housekeeping State, as
distinct from the police State, could already faintly be discerned. It was natural that, once the books on Trade Unionism
were out of the way, their authors should regard as their next
most urgent task the study of local government. They had
begun with the intention of limiting their work to the problems
of their own day, and of dispatching in a preliminary chapter
the age before 1835; but they found the hand of the past too
heavy to be shaken off. The period finally chosen was that in
which local administrators found themselves confronted, as a
result of rapid economic change, with problems of a new
complexity, which they were left to solve or ignore as they
themselves deemed best, unaided and unimpeded, save on
rare occasions, by the intervention of the central government.
Except for the volumes on the Poor Law, which began earlier
and ended later, it was the century and a half between 1688
and the partial reconstruction of local institutions which
followed the first Reform Act.

*English Local Government from the Revolution to the Municipal
Corporations Act* was begun in 1898; the last instalment of it to
be published appeared in 1930. The plan, as first conceived,
was not carried to completion. Public duties intervened; and

H

some subjects on which the authors had intended to write, such as the Suppression of Nuisances, the Provision of Markets, and the Regulation of Trade, had to be left for treatment by other hands. The four volumes on the structure of local government, and the six dealing with its functions, include, however, the greater part of the original design. The best introduction to the series as a whole is contained in the two concluding chapters of *Statutory Authorities for Special Purposes*—the cheerless title of a great book—which Mrs. Webb regarded as "the most intellectually distinguished" of their works. It is in these *ad hoc* bodies, established under local acts for sewering, paving, draining, lighting, and policing the rapidly growing towns of an insanitary and disorderly age, rather than in institutions, like the borough, of greater antiquity and fame, that the Webbs find the germ of the municipal and county government of today. The story of the transition, as they tell it, is one, not merely of the elaboration of machinery, but of the emergence of new principles. The substitution of the citizen-consumer, as the controlling power in local government, for the vocational organisations of agriculturists, traders, and craftsmen; of election for self-appointment or co-option; of the contractor employing hired labour for the obligation of gratuitous service; of salaried officials for the freehold tenure of profitable office; of the increasing intervention of departments of the central government for the almost unchecked predominance of local custom and the common law—such, they suggest, are the high landmarks on the road from the old order to the new.

On the validity of their conclusions, as on the details of their narrative, only a specialist can venture to speak. The layman will linger with sympathy, and sometimes with amusement, over the human elements in their story. The members of their local bodies breathe, move, and labour; plan for the public good, and sometimes for their own; toil selflessly for lofty ends; intrigue, swallow bribes, and engage, in Fielding's words, in "plots and circumventions, parties and factions, equal to those which are to be found in courts." The boss of Bethnal Green, a picture after Hogarth; the select vestry of St. George's Hanover Square, never known to levy an illegal rate or to indulge in convivialities at the public expense; justices who are devoted reformers, like Sir George Paul in Gloucestershire or Thomas

Bailey in Lancashire, and the magistrates of the Middlesex
Bench, whom Burke described as the scum of the earth; the
precocious municipal democracy of Norwich, sinking into an
orgy of corrupt and violent party politics; the rulers of the tiny
town of Tetbury, blameless as the Ethiopians, who, having
purchased the manor from its impecunious lord, administer
the property as a trust for the benefit, not only of the freemen,
but of all the inhabitants, persuade the commoners to allow
their pastures to be ploughed for wheat till the debt is paid off,
and actually induce them to permit all immigrants into the
borough to enjoy, after the lapse of seven years, the same
privileges as themselves—these portraits, lovable, scandalous,
or comic, are a small selection from a large gallery. Local
government is interpreted throughout in a broad sense. The
student seeking for light on the management of open-field
farming, the part played by gilds in municipal life, the problems
arising when villages were converted into towns unequipped
with the apparatus of an urban civilisation, or the Poor Law
history of the last quarter of a century, which the authors helped
to make as well as to write, will not be disappointed. Not all
their judgments will command assent; but here, as elsewhere,
they put their cards on the table, and are at pains to provide
the means of confirming or refuting their interpretations. The
reader of their volumes, who stands back and considers the
work as a whole, is likely to feel that he has been in contact with
the history, not merely of English local government, but of the
English people.

The Webbs were generally regarded, both in this country
and abroad, as the intellectual leaders of British Socialism. The
small number of their books specifically devoted to that subject
may, at first sight, cause surprise. They had, as they wrote in
1921, "been investigating and describing democratic institutions
for nearly thirty years" before they "published any volume
dealing with national government or the political State"; and,
neither then nor later, did the topics to which some Socialist
thinkers have devoted a large space figure prominently in their
pages. The truth is that their approach, not only to Socialism,
but to economic issues in general, took a different line from
that previously followed by most theorists, whether to right or
left. Mrs. Webb has explained in her autobiography the

reasons which led her, at an early stage of her career, to the view that the province of political economy, as commonly conceived in her youth, required to be redefined. They regarded the economics of profit-making capitalism—one of a long series of different methods which men had employed for organising the production of wealth—as an important subject of study side by side with other social institutions; but they thought that analysis, in order to be fruitful, must go hand in hand with investigation. They were out of sympathy, therefore, both with the tradition of abstract speculation which descended from Ricardo and with the attempt of some Socialists to turn its batteries against itself by employing, as in the case of the labour theory of value, analogous methods to create a system of counter-doctrine. Dialectical materialism left them equally sceptical. "If," they drily remark, "there is any such influence at work, it is naturally a fit subject for objective study, together with the phenomena themselves. To us 'the materialist conception of history' is merely one hypothesis among many . . . which, like all hypotheses, may be useful as an instrument of investigation, but acquires scientific value only in so far as it is verified by an objective observation of the facts."

Their own attitude to questions of social policy was realist, experimental, and constructive. It resulted from the habits formed and lessons learned during their long career as students and administrators. Holding that light, not heat, was the world's chief need, and believing that reason and goodwill would, if given time, prevail, they were impatient of criticisms without affirmations, and refused to preach ideals till they had found the way to realise them. They thought it more important to interpret the trends of social development, and to prescribe, after careful diagnosis, specific remedies for particular evils, than to appeal to the appetite for emotionalism or system-mongering.

Mrs. Webb, while still Miss Potter, had been impressed by the fact that the class in which she was brought up "habitually gave orders, but . . . seldom, if ever, executed the orders of other people." The problem, as she and her husband saw it, was to substitute for that unconscious dictatorship of the capitalist, with the capricious inequalities and irresponsible power which appeared to them to result from it, arrangements permitting the effective participation of ordinary men and women in the conduct of the economic affairs on which their livelihood depended. Capitalism, they argued in *The Decline of Capitalist Civilisation*, had rendered genuine services in awakening dormant energies, and canalising them, with profit as the magnet, for the production of wealth; but its cost in human suffering and degradation—a degradation not confined to the losers in the struggle—had been heavy. Till recently, a practicable alternative to it had been difficult to state. Now, thanks to the growth of new forms of social organisation and to the administrative experience gained in the last half-century, it was possible to do better. The collective regulation of private industry, with its tentative approach to the establishment of minimum standards of civilised existence; the collective administration, by municipalities and the State, of an increasing number of services; the extension of communal provision for the needs of the young, the sick, the aged, and the unemployed; and the development of progressive taxation—not to mention, what they regarded as of equal importance, the growth of Co-operation and Trade Unionism—were creating, even before 1914, a society markedly different from that which they had known in their youth. It was by progress along these lines—progress rapid and deliberate, instead of halting and haphazard—that the goal at which they aimed was, they thought, to be attained.

Such views exposed flanks to attack from opposite extremes. They did not fail to receive it. An accusation whose validity the authors would not have admitted is that, perhaps, most often brought against them. It is the charge of a bureaucratic indifference to individual freedom. They would have replied to it that liberty means, not the right of particular individuals of groups to use as they may think fit such power as past history and present social arrangements may happen to have conferred on them, but the establishment of conditions promoting "the utmost possible development of faculty" in all human beings, and that liberty, in that sense, has law as its mother. In an urban and industrial civilisation the alternative to planning by a democratic State for the general good was not, it seemed to them, the freedom of every individual to arrange his own affairs as best suited himself. It was the acquiescence,

under economic duress, of the mass of mankind in an environment and style of life created by the self-interest of powerful
minorities. The freedom of the majority had been substantially
increased since the middle of last century by the development
of various forms of collective control, which the interests
opposed to them had at first denounced as tyranny. Its further
extension would take place by analogous methods. It required
for its enlargement not less public action, but more.

It is not surprising, therefore, that the aspect of the Soviet
social order which most aroused the Webbs' enthusiasm should
have been, neither the first turbulent phase, nor the brief
essay in syndicalism, but the subsequent "deliberate planning
of all the nation's production, distribution and exchange, not
for the profit of the few, but for increasing the consumption
of the whole community." They had read, before their visit,
almost everything written on Soviet Russia in English, French,
and German; nor were they unacquainted with the considerable
literature expounding the objections, economic and political,
to the principle of a planned economy. In the two volumes
of *Soviet Communism* they state their own conclusions. They
thought that the system worked, that it had raised the low
standard of life of the Russian people, and that it was not
threatened with an internal breakdown. They thought also
that, in spite of the absence of Western democratic forms, it
rested on a broad basis of popular support, which found
expression through a wide range of different organs, and that
it owed its achievements partly to the determination of its
rulers to make the fullest use of scientific knowledge, partly
to its success in evoking among the mass of the population a
spirit of service and solidarity to which capitalist societies,
with their emphasis on the motive of pecuniary self-interest,
were precluded from appealing in equal measure. Whether
their book will survive, like de Tocqueville's *Democracy in
America*, as the most illuminating of contemporary pictures of
a new society in the making, time alone can show. Whatever
the verdict upon it, it remains an impressive attempt by two
experienced sociologists, who were neither innocents nor
fanatics, to interpret to their fellow-countrymen an unfamiliar
civilisation.

III

It was of the nature of the studies which the Webbs made
their own, as well as of their personal convictions, that knowledge and its application should go hand in hand. Their
books were not the harvest of a life of leisure. They were
written, and should be read, as the product, not only of
scholarship, but of the civic temper. At the time when their
joint work began, Mr. Webb, through his position on the
London County Council, was deeply involved in the educational politics of the day, including the reform of the University
of London and the discussions preceding the Education Act of
1902. Mrs. Webb, since her evidence before the Lords' Committee on Sweating, had been known as a woman who could
be relied on to handle thorny questions with candour and
without sentiment. Both had their own projects, which they
wished to serve; but both were recognised to be personally
disinterested, to be free from Party attachments, and to care
not at all, provided that the work which they thought necessary
was done, what Government or individual received the credit
for doing it. Miss Haldane, the sister of their oldest friend in
public life, has remarked on the influence which came to them
from their political catholicity. The comment is just.

The claims on Mrs. Webb were not of a kind which can be
neatly tabulated, but neither were they light. From the time
when, in the nineties, she was coaching Trade Union members
of the Labour Commission, advising Conservative acquaintances on the Factory Bill in 1895, and helping her husband
to float the newly founded London School of Economics and
Political Science—their chief venture of those years—over the
shoals which beset its youth, down to her service on the Reconstruction Committee and her assistance in the twenties to the
reorganised Labour Party, she was rarely without some cause
which needed nursing on her hands. She never abandoned her
long-term research; but there were periods when it had to
take a second place. The five and a half years devoted to Poor
Law reform were the longest of them. She had become a
member of the Royal Commission on the Poor Laws appointed
in December 1905, and, down to January 1909, when it
reported, she gave her whole time to it. She resisted the dis-

position of some of her colleagues to collect opinions instead
of facts; insisted that expert assistants should be appointed to
make detailed reports on different topics of importance; and
carried out, with the aid of her secretaries, several inquiries
of her own into subjects on which she thought further information was required. The Minority Report signed by herself and
three other commissioners, of which she and her husband were
joint authors, while it naturally encountered opposition, was,
by general consent, an impressive achievement. The knowledge
behind it was not open to question, but its grasp of Poor Law
history and administration was less important than its constructive proposals. By challenging the principle of an authority
whose functions were confined to the relief of destitution, and
insisting that the duty of the State was, not merely to alleviate
distress, but to grapple with its causes, it shook an ancient
problem out of the ruts of the past, and lifted the discussion
of policy on to a new plane.

The Commission involved some hard fighting, as well as
steady labour. It left Mrs. Webb temporarily worn out. Its
sequel was not less exhausting. Hitherto, though strenuous in
work behind the scenes, she had shunned publicity. The
campaign for the break-up of the Poor Law was her first and
only plunge into agitation on the grand scale. For more than
two years, from the spring of 1909 to the summer of 1911,
her whole energy was given to organisation and propaganda.
Backed by a National Committee representing all parties and
denominations, and including men and women eminent in
many different walks of life, the Webbs raised money, maintained an active and well-staffed central office, established
branches, conducted a journal, arranged conferences and
lectures, and themselves toured the country, Mrs. Webb
sometimes speaking four or five times a week. The agitation
cost them some friends, and was not immediately successful.
Other plans found favour in high places, and the insurance
legislation temporarily diverted public attention. A sub-committee of the Reconstruction Committee endorsed in 1918 the
main proposals of the Minority Report; but action did not
follow. It was not till 1929, when the authorship of the
proposal had been almost forgotten, that the Local Government Act of that year wound up the Boards of Guardians,

and transferred their functions to the councils of counties and
county boroughs.

The struggle for the reform of the Poor Laws was the heaviest
piece of public work which Mrs. Webb undertook. In the
breathing-space which followed it, in addition to publishing a
further volume of *English Local Government*, she and her husband
launched two new ventures. The period of acute industrial
conflict from 1910 to 1914 was marked by the emergence of
issues which, if not novel in principle, had not previously been
formulated with equal sharpness. The attitude of the Webbs
to the policies epitomised as "workers' control," of which
much was to be heard during the following decade, was a
combination of interested scepticism as to the practicability of
the programme with a resolute determination to remain on
cordial terms with its advocates. Not less characteristically,
they insisted that, whatever the merits of the doctrines advanced, the first essential was, not controversy or propaganda,
but a dispassionate study of the industrial structure to which
the new prescriptions were to be applied. The Fabian Research
Department, founded on the initiative of Mrs. Webb, was
intended to be an organ of unemotional knowledge. The *New
Statesman*—during the first years of its existence an uncon-
ventional journal, which united with the ordinary functions of
a weekly the publication of massive supplements on social
subjects—was to diffuse light, as it grew, among wider circles
than could be reached by books.

The war, whose outbreak found the Webbs at work on
investigations into the Control of Industry, Insurance, and the
Organisation of the Professions, brought new duties. Mrs.
Webb served on a series of official committees, including the
Statutory Pensions Committee, which dealt with the pensions
of disabled soldiers; the Reconstruction Committee established
in 1917, where she piloted the proposals of the Minority
Report on the Poor Laws through a sub-committee on problems
of local government, and helped, as member of another sub-
committee presided over by Lord Haldane, to produce a
notable report on the Machinery of Central Government; and
the Committee on Women in Industry. The subject referred by
the War Cabinet to the last body—the relation between the
wages of men and women—has not ceased to perplex. The

analysis of the problem contained in her Minority Report is not yet out of date.

By the time that it appeared obligations of an unexpected kind were beginning to descend upon her and her husband. They had been members of the Labour Party since its foundation, and had maintained friendly relations with its leaders, as with those of other parties. Regarding, however, the promotion of social and economic knowledge as their principal task, they had turned a deaf ear to appeals to enter politics. The new situation which, it was evident, would develop on the return of peace caused a reluctant change of mind. From 1918, when Mr. Webb stood as candidate for the University of London, and still more from 1922, when he entered Parliament as member for Seaham Harbour, the attempt to assist the Labour Party to become an effective political force was, next to his duties as a Minister and the completion of their books, the Webbs' main pre-occupation. Mrs. Webb, who was not a lover of the ritualism of politics, evaded merely ceremonial claims as best she could; but she took seriously the practical obligations of political life, keeping closely in touch, by lectures and correspondence, with the women in her husband's constituency; serving on the Advisory Committees of the Party; attending international Socialist conferences at Hamburg and Geneva; and making their house in London a centre where members and leaders could meet in a congenial atmosphere. Their literary work was, doubtless, slowed down; but they were masters of the art of canalising their energies, and it suffered less than might have been expected. The strenuous phase of the parliamentary episode lasted for nine years, during just under three of which one of the partners was in office. The three volumes of *English Local Government*, which, together with *My Apprenticeship*, were published during that period, do not suggest that they were composed in haste or by hands that had lost their cunning. Eight months after the election of 1931, in May 1932, the two authors, he seventy-three and she seventy-four, set out for Russia.

IV

Some of the problems discussed by the Webbs in their earlier works are, partly thanks to them, less urgent than they were. They were those of a generation impressed by the spectacle of a rapid increase in wealth, and disposed to believe, if with diminishing assurance, that positive measures to cure social evils were rendered superfluous by the certainty of its continuance. Neither Mrs. Webb nor her husband cherished sentimental illusions as to the unimportance of material progress. So far, indeed, from endorsing the view that "the problem of production has been solved," they were appalled by the inefficiency with which man's struggle with nature is often conducted. What distinguished them from most of their contemporaries who were interested in the same subjects was not merely their rejection of the doctrine, in the nineties still a power, that "the answer to the question 'how to make the nation rich' is 'by letting each member of it make himself as rich as he can in his own way.' " It was their grasp of the truth that social processes, in order to be controlled, must be known thoroughly and in detail, and the inexhaustible energy, sustained for half a century, which they brought to the investigation of them.

The conception of a social order planned, with general consent, for the common good has a long history behind it; but earlier prophets of the destination had rarely mapped the roads. The Webbs were strong where their predecessors had been weak. Prescription not preceded by diagnosis appeared to them charlatanism, and diagnosis was a task to which virtuous intentions were less important than a sound technique. "Only by watching the *processes* of decay and growth over a period of time," wrote Mrs. Webb, "can we understand even the contemporary facts . . . and only by such a comprehension of the past and present processes can we get an insight into the means of change." Hence their long list of works on particular topics, and their refusal to formulate a political philosophy except by way of comment on the specific subject in hand. Hence also their view of the path which reform must tread. Their gradualism was not, as was absurdly suggested, the statement of a preference, as though loitering were their

favourite foible, but a recognition of the facts of a world where
life is lived in time. They were the last persons to wait on
events, when it was in their power to accelerate them; and
for the authors of real changes, whether small or great, whether
a clause in a Factory Act or a Five Years' Plan, they had a
profound respect; but they were free from the illusion—odd,
though not uncommon—that barking is synonymous with
biting, and were aware of the truth not always remembered
that the latter operation, in order to become effective,
requires that, at some stage of the proceedings, open mouths
should be shut. They were not, therefore, of the intellectuals
who see in the Labour Movement a substitute for the cinema,
and who relapse into paroxysms of grief, scorn, and indignation
at its lamentable indifference to their appetite for melodrama.
They thought that invention and construction—the production,
as they put it, of "new social tissue"—not denunciation or
demolition, were the root of the matter. Romantic revolu-
tionaries, all rhetoric and blank cartridges, usually bored, and
sometimes irritated, them.

Their long years of labour, and the persistence with which,
unmoved by changing fashions, they held on their course,
gave them the air of an institution. Disliking sciolism, they
were cautious in expressing opinions on matters outside their
own field. On those within it, the perplexed inquirer, whether
student, official, trade unionist, or politician, could appeal to
them as an oracle, returning with collective wisdom—"we
think"—unambiguous answers from a wealth of experience no
one else could command. The comparison of them with
Bentham is, in that respect, apt; but if, like the sage, they
were a fountain of ideas, they had none of his eccentricity,
and more than his humanity. Of the legends that gathered
about them, some hit off salient traits, but most missed the
mark. The noblest of all titles, they used to say, is that of
servant, and "the firm of Webb" served public causes with a
concentration of purpose which few men bring to their own;
but the partners were neither a card-index of facts nor bleak
and arid doctrinaires. Their influence was not confined to their
public activities, and they impressed those who knew them not
less by what they were than by what they did. When at work,
they drove themselves hard; but they were not righteous over-

much and knew how to be busy without being hurried. To visit them at Passfield Corner, or to spend with them part of the holidays which they were fabled never to take, was to share the company of two sociable personalities, with a psychological curiosity not too elevated to enjoy gossip, an engaging capacity for laughing at themselves, and the appetite for physical exercise of a gryphon in the wilderness.

Of the characteristics which they had in common, simplicity and magnanimity were, perhaps, the most striking. The combination of worldly wisdom with personal unworldliness, though rare, is not unknown. The Webbs possessed it in more than ordinary measure. While they knew exactly what they wanted, and had few rivals in the business of "getting things done," their achievements owed more to single-mindedness and integrity than to the artful astuteness ascribed to them by the credulous. Some hard knocks came their way, not only from opponents; but to bear no grudges was part of their creed. It was easy to disagree with them, but difficult to stage a quarrel, and, when friends insisted on nursing a grievance, they were indefatigable in seeking opportunities to reforge broken links. To the young they were charming; smoothing their way to useful work; treating them as colleagues, not as disciples; and weighing the criticisms of the rebels who ridiculed them with a seriousness the more disarming because prompted, not merely by a desire to spare sensitive feelings, but by the assumption of an equality of interest in the advancement of the common cause. Like others, who did not share their political opinions, they were shocked, if not greatly surprised, by the sins against light which followed the first war. Believers themselves in persuasion by an appeal to reason, they discerned symptoms of a growing disposition to stop ears and close minds, which seemed to them ominous, and their later writings sound a note of warning not heard in their earlier. They never lost, however, their faith in public spirit guided by knowledge as the architect of a better world. Their old age was free from disillusionment or cynicism. The Order of Merit conferred on Lord Passfield for "eminent services to Social and Political Science" was an appropriate tribute to that part of their joint work to which Mrs. Webb, as well as her husband, attached most importance.

In lives so united individual contributions are not easily distinguished. It was not a case, as is sometimes suggested, of a division of labour between theorist and investigator or inventor and executant, or of flashes of creative insight later turned into generalisations which would stand criticism and plans which would march. The ideas of the partners were struck out in a continuous duologue, in which each was flint and steel in turn. The impression of a listener was rather of one complex personality communing with itself than of two debating with each other. The individuality of each, however, had its characteristic traits, the expression of a distinct psychological background. Their intellectual approach to problems was usually the same. In their emotional reactions to them they sometimes differed. The union of identity of purpose with diversity of temperament was part of their strength.

The Beatrice Webb of fiction, a combination of economic pedant with hard woman of affairs, did not survive the publication of *My Apprenticeship*. It is evident from her account of her early life that she was exceptionally sensitive and highly strung, with an artist's eye for the subtleties of individual character, and an unusual power of expressing them. The imagination to which collective humanity is as real and moving as individuals who are seen is not a common faculty. She possessed it to an extraordinary degree. "To me," she once wrote, after quoting some lines by Sir Ronald Ross, the discoverer of the cause of malaria, "a million sick have always seemed actually more worthy of sympathy than 'the child sick in a fever' preferred by Mrs. Browning's Aurora Leigh." Her early contacts with scientists strongly influenced her thought; but it was her imaginative grasp of the lot of unknown lives, rather than intellectual curiosity, which first turned her to sociology.

Once sure of her vocation, she mastered its methods by a long and painful conflict, disciplining her intellect and canalising her emotions with an intensity of effort which, to judge by her diary, sometimes brought her near despair. Her touch of ascetic austerity, as of a Puritan casting behind him all impediments to his quest, was partly the legacy of that early struggle to subdue herself, partly the expression of a philosophy which disliked emphasis on the externals of life—luxury, ostentation,

and the claims of pampered classes to special consideration—
both as bad manners and as a source of social corruption.
Her demands on brain and will were exacting; but she was
not of the reformers who are intolerable in private life, nor did
she, as some observers thought, live solely for her work. She
diffused warmth, as well as light, and was quick, amid all her
preoccupations, to offer sympathy, encouragement, and wise
counsel to individuals in need of them. Acquaintances, to
whom her intellectual eminence meant little, described her as
the kindest woman they had ever met. She thought companion-
ship the most delightful form of happiness, and welcomed it
with open arms.

In trying, as occasionally she did, to formulate her own
creed, she underlined the distinction between the spheres of
means and ends, of machinery and purpose, of organisation
and the spirit. In the first she was a rationalist, severely critical
of her own work, and impatient of sentimentality, slipshod
argument, and dilettantism. In the second she was a mystic.
"The habit of prayer," she wrote, in describing some difficult
years of early womanhood, "enabled me to survive, and
to emerge relatively sound in body and sane in mind." It
remained with her throughout life. After one of the opening
sessions of the Commission on the Poor Laws, feeling her
responsibilities heavy on her, she went to St. Paul's to pray,
and she continued the practice at intervals during the period
of its sittings. In the reflections on the study of society recently
quoted by Professor Powicke from *My Apprenticeship*, two voices
answer each other:

"This ceaseless questioning of social facts," the Ego that denies
was always insisting, "seems an interesting way of passing the time,
but does it lead anywhere?"

The Ego that affirms could now answer with confidence:

"Seeing that society is one vast laboratory in which experiments
in human relationship, conscious or unconscious, careless or deliberate, are continuously being carried on, those races will survive and
prosper which are equipped with the knowledge of how things
happen. And this knowledge can only be acquired by persistent
research into the past and present behaviour of man."

"How things happen!" mocks the Ego that denies, "but that does
not settle what *ought* to happen."

"I thought I told you long ago," calmly answers the Ego that affirms, "that, with regard to the purpose of life, science is and must remain bankrupt; and the men of science of to-day know it. . . . How each of us determines our scale of values no one knows. For my own part, I find it best to live 'as if' the soul of man were in communion with a superhuman force which makes for righteousness. Like our understanding of nature through observation and reasoning, this communion with the spirit of love at work in the universe will be intermittent and incomplete, and it will frequently fail us. But a failure to know, and the fall from grace, is the way of all flesh."

9

The Webbs and their Work[1]

THE topic on which I have been asked to speak requires no apology, but I approach it with some diffidence. There are many in my audience who knew the Webbs too well to require an account of them; nor am I sure that the indefatigable lecturers, who are the subject of my remarks, would have enjoyed being turned into the text for a lecture. They submitted patiently to publicity, as to everything else, when the cause required it, and no one knew better, if lime-light was the order of the day, what buttons to press; but they were not lovers of honorific ritual. Their air, when the thing was over, was, "There, that's done; now for something serious." I suspect that they would have regarded an address devoted to themselves as among the emotional substitutes for work which they were accustomed to dismiss, in their more frivolous moments, under the name of "religious exercises."

So my sensations are much what they were when, as a youth who had not yet got over his education, I paid my first visit to 41 Grosvenor Road, and was so unfortunate as to depart with the headgear of another guest. I felt, as a more than ordinarily massive bowler settled heavily on my shoulders, a momentary surprise; but I had not yet learned from my hosts that investigation, measurement, and verification are among the first duties of man, and I assumed, with the casual optimism of youth, that, though the incubus seemed unfamiliar, it would come all right somehow. It was not till next morning

[1] Webb Memorial Lecture, May 1945. Parts of the lecture have been omitted, as they dealt with topics touched on in the obituary of Mrs. Webb, and certain supplementary matter has been added to it.

that a scorching letter from Mrs. Webb informed me that I had eloped with the property of one whom I hope it is not disrespectful to describe as taking, in all senses of the expression, an out-size in hats, the then about to be Right Honourable John Burns, over whom at the moment she was casting her flies, and was anxious to retain in a humour to swallow them. The episode confirmed her conviction of the incorrigible incompetence, unreliability, moral laxity, and mental imbecility of most products, however insignificant, of the older universities, and took some years to live down. I feel now somewhat the same embarrassment as I experienced then, an embarrassment at once softened and reinforced by later memories, as though Beatrice, her skirts turned back and crouching over the fire, were ejaculating into one ear, "Beware of dilettantism," and Sidney, full-length on the sofa, were murmuring into the other, "Above all, no intimacies."

The latter injunction I propose to follow. In the library of hell a special stack is reserved for those biographies—a vast and dreary host—of great men and women, which throw light on every aspect of their victims' personalities, from their taste in dress to their second cousins' Christian names, except the characteristics in which their greatness consisted. I should be sorry to add another item to it. It must suffice to say that the conventional caricature of Sidney as a bureaucratic energumen, all pigeon-holes and statistics, is as remote from reality as the austere *virago* who, before the appearance of *My Apprenticeship*, passed for poor Beatrice. In reality, he was a man of unusual breadth of culture; widely read, not only in the English, but in the French and German, literature of his large range of subjects; and with a grasp of the ends which the machine exists to serve which caused him, when asked the name of the greatest Socialist he had known, to give, without a moment's hestitation, the unexpected answer, William Morris. Together, when off duty, they were known to their friends as two sociable people, delighting in casual conversation, easily amused, and with an appetite on the part of one partner for physical exercise, defended by her with arguments, hygienic and ethical, of terrifying cogency, against which the other periodically rebelled, but always, in my experience, rebelled in vain.

They are also, however, historical figures, and figures whose stature increases as their world recedes. They faced great issues, and grappled with them in a great way. They changed thought and action. They founded new institutions and launched ideas which remade old ones. They conquered for knowledge and made habitable for men departments of social life which, before them, were a trackless jungle. They forced upon national attention the importance of movements which today are a power, but which, till the Webbs' searchlight was turned on them, still awaited recognition; revealed their significance to a public sceptical and often hostile; and charted some segments of their course to their goal. They researched, wrote, agitated, administered and—since only the last stages of legislation take place in Parliament—were not the less legislators because, save for ten years when both of them were over sixty, County Hall and the British Museum saw more of them than the House of Commons.

The study of social institutions with a view to transforming them, which was their special sphere of work, does not lend itself to treatment in terms of the spectacular exploits of extraordinary individuals. But there is authority for the statement that the serpent on the rock is as miraculous in his own way, as the eagle in the air; and what the Webbs' unflagging war on ignorance, apathy, and prejudice may lack in drama it gains in the impressiveness of positive accomplishment. If a man looks back on the successive chapters of British social history from 1880 to 1930—if he reflects on such movements as Trade Unionism, Co-operation, and the rise of the Labour Party; or considers, in another sphere, industrial policy, financial policy, public education and public health, unemployment, the Poor Law, the development of municipal enterprise and Local Government in general; or ponders the advance in civilisation which the changed public attitude to all these subjects represents—he is unlikely, I think, to conclude that the patient labourers ploughed the sands. He will find few problems which they failed to illumine, few abuses against which their blows were not the heaviest struck, few reforms in which they did not play a decisive, if often a deliberately self-effacing, part. Whatever our individual interests and creeds—whether we are active workers in social movements, or merely students of them, or ordinary citizens concerned for decency, good sense and fair play in the management of our common concerns—we are all their pupils. The authors of such achievements have no need of the small change of reminiscences to perpetuate their memory. The noblest of all titles, they used to say, is that of servant. The legacy, scientific and practical, of their half-century of devoted labour is the monument by which we may most fittingly recall them.

If the work of the Webbs is too massive for biographical gossip, an attempt to provide them with intellectual ancestors is equally superfluous. Historians of political thought are apt to be obsessed with origins and pedigrees, as though ideas were transmitted in the same manner as property, and different attitudes to society and theories about it succeeded each other by direct descent. To most of us, who take our views at second-hand, that procedure may apply. Where creative minds are concerned, it is absurdly off the mark. Original people are not links in a chain; more often they are breaks in one. Presented with the metaphorical torch which each generation is supposed to hand on to the next, they insist on making certain that it is what it is alleged to be. If it turns out on investigation, as not infrequently it does, to be, not an authentic illuminant, but a smelly taper, they incontinently blow it out, and proceed to replace it with lamps of their own. The Webbs were voracious readers, endowed with memories of embarrassing efficiency, which armed them with precedents for every innovation, and rarely left them at a loss for apt quotations from authors who would have trembled with apprehension at the alarming causes that they were cited to support. But they possessed—a quality which all readers should have, and most of us have not—a high degree of resisting power. They took from the predecessors hints which served their purpose, and let the rest slide off them. The clue to their outlook on the world of their day is to be found less in what they absorbed of its prevalent assumptions and fashionable philosophies than in what they ignored or dropped into the dust-bin.

Their position is not to be understood, therefore, by analysing it into elements derived from different sources. It was too much their own. It is interesting that Beatrice should have been brought up in an atmosphere compounded of London Society, country houses, and the Big Business which kept both the merry-go-rounds spinning; that she should have mixed from childhood with the scientists and men of letters whom her father, a civilised capitalist, invited to his house; and that the most intimate of her parents' friends, at whose feet for a time she sat, should have been that forgotten celebrity, Herbert Spencer. It is more significant that at twenty-five she had outgrown him, and that the influence which finally clinched her decision to devote her life to social research came, not from books or teachers, but from sympathies aroused and lessons learned on the occasion of a month's visit to some Lancashire cousins, who, when her own branch of the family had been wafted upwards, had remained operatives at Bacup. It is interesting that Sidney should have been nurtured on the purest milk of Victorian radicalism; that he should have attended lectures on Natural Science by Huxley—an occasion on which, since the course was confined to workers in industry, he put down his trade as that of a wood-carver, on the ground that he would carve if he could—that the only contemporary economist whom he respected should have been Mill, with whose deductions from Ricardo's theory of rent he later himself did much execution; and that he should have thought that, if a theory of value was necessary to salvation, the article supplied by Jevons was, on the whole, a less unhandy instrument than that of Marx. It is more significant that, at an age when most well-to-do young people have not left the university, he had seen the inside of a broker's office in the City and of three Government Departments; that his first paper to the Fabian Society, at the age of twenty-six, had the characteristically curt and trenchant title, *The Way Out*; and that, when offered Liberal constituencies to stop his mouth, he decided that there was more both to be done and to be learned on the L.C.C. than in Parliament.

The truth is that neither of our friends was of the kind which is disposed to take opinions from a master. Each of them independently had gone young through the business of settling accounts with current cant, whether to right or left, which is the necessary preliminary to serious work. Apart from the influence of science, in whose disciplined attack on its problems they saw an example for sociologists, both of them owed more to experience than to the doctrines of the schools. One partner, according to his own account, had been converted to Socialism by a lecturer at Birkbeck College, an otherwise unknown Mr. Smith. As, however, what convinced him of the virtues of nationalisation, and set him agog to propound plans for applying it, was the fatuity of the arguments advanced by Mr. Smith against it, his debt to his teacher was more negative than positive, and he is not an example of the docile disciple. The abandonment by the other of a creed which she described as "agnosticism tempered by individualist economics" was slower and more painful. It had begun, to her own surprise, in the course of her collaboration with Booth in his *The Life and Labour of the People of London*. It had taken place, in all but name, before she had completed her book on Co-operation.

Both possessed the fire at the centre without which great things are not done; but, having made up their minds on first principles, they took their work too seriously to be emotional about it, and there is a sense in which the fact that they were Socialists is less important than the kind of Socialists they were. They looked at facts through plain glass; held that light, not heat, was the world's main need; saw no reason why the devil should have a monopoly of the business virtues; and thought that Capitalism was most likely to be brought to terms, not by blowing trumpets round its walls, but by mobilising against it, not only the qualities which it despised, but also the organising ability and concentrated effort which were its special boast. They regarded the Co-operative Commonwealth neither as a distant Utopia, nor as the inevitable climax of an irresistible evolution, but as an edifice to be built piecemeal by hard, practical labour, an edifice which—since its building was a long-term job—should be begun here and now, and to the erection of which system, method, application, technical skill, a reasonable consideration for the prejudices and susceptibilities of ordinary men and women, and above all, knowledge, were not less indispensable than enthusiasm and eloquence. Their first contributions to that programme were made when they were under thirty. They were continuing to make them when they were both over eighty.

Their business, as they saw it when they joined forces in 1892, was pioneering on two fronts. The first essential was to know exactly and in detail what required to be done; the second to mobilise the energy to do it, which meant, till the distant day when a Government of their own persuasion should be in power, the education of public opinion and the instruction of politicians in matters about which both at the time were ill-informed, and the latter, when not actively hostile, were commonly indifferent. They approached that task from slightly different angles. Mrs. Webb's introduction to economic questions had been that of an investigator, not of a propagandist. She joined the Fabian Society in 1893, but a long interval elapsed before she played an active part in it. For a decade following her marriage, she remained primarily a student, though a student who found in the service of social causes the inspiration to her work. Her husband, after ten years in the Colonial Office, to which a generation later he returned as Minister, had been elected to the London County Council in 1892. As chairman of its Technical Education Committee, into whose orbit he contrived to sweep, much to the advantage of the service, almost the whole of London's higher education, he was a busy administrator, though an administrator with a profound conviction of the dependence of social progress on systematic research and the application of its results. But they saw theory and practice as complementary aspects—the staff-work and operations—of a single campaign. Each laboured unceasingly and simultaneously at both, and both threw their whole selves into each. The London School of Economics, the chief venture of their early years, was designed by them, not as a cloistered college, but as a mundane institution around which should eddy the full tide and roar of London life. The supercilious description of it given by a denizen of a more secluded university—"one of those places like Selfridge's, isn't it?"—though its hint of financial prosperity is unfortunately unfounded, conveys a suggestion of workman-like realism which the founders of the School, so far from resenting, would have welcomed as a compliment. If, therefore, I touch separately on their literary work and their practical activities, the reason is not that they themselves distinguished between them. It is merely considerations of practical convenience.

The first publications of both the authors appeared in the same year, when, in 1887, one produced the first edition of

Facts for Socialists, and the other an article on *The Dock Life of East London*. The last, a joint-work, *The Truth about Soviet Russia*, was published in 1942. In the intervening half-century, they were together responsible, usually as partners, for some forty-five volumes, apart from a long list of pamphlets—Webb produced not less than forty-seven for the Fabian Society alone —articles, essays and introductions to books composed by other writers. Their more important works may be classified, perhaps, into five main groups. They include four books on working-class organisation and policy; ten volumes on English Local Government; four substantial works and various shorter pieces on the reform of the Poor Laws; four books—two of them by Sidney alone and two of them by both together—specifically devoted to Socialism; and a group of miscellaneous writings, of which the most striking are *My Apprenticeship*, the elaborate study of *Soviet Communism*, and the two shorter books on the same subject which followed it.

Continuous labour by two busy people on so ambitious a scale demanded system and method. They were assisted by secretaries, their one extravagance—there was a period when, it is said, they found work for six at once—but they did not spare themselves. A breadth of intensive research, which few scraps of evidence escape; an unusual power of illuminating generalisation; a measured force of argument which strikes home to the mind with a kind of inevitability as though what was speaking were the voice, not of two fallible mortals, but of Society herself, instructing her foolish children how to live at peace—such are the qualities, the fruits of an immense effort of self-discipline, which cause the Webbs' major works to stand out, amid the trivialities of their day and ours, like Roman masonry in a London suburb. The classics devoted to Trade Unionism and Local Government reveal them at their best.

The former, for their significance to be appreciated, must be seen against the background of the age instructed by them. In the nineties of last century the right of professional association was secure on the statute-book; but a generation had elapsed without the moral being drawn. Public ignorance of the objects and methods of trade unions; a prejudice slow to die among economists; misrepresentation in the Press; persecution by employers outside the staple industries; a hostility on the part of the Courts that they hardly troubled to conceal, all worked in one direction. They combined to perpetuate in late-Victorian England an attitude to organised Labour somewhat resembling that prevalent down to 1935 in the United States; and deeper depths than that no mortal eye can plumb. To suggest that this mountainous load of uninformed or interested opposition could have been rolled back by two books, or, indeed, by any dynamic less powerful than its victims' will to freedom would be, no doubt, absurd; but what authors could do the Webbs did, and did superbly. The *History of Trade Unionism* showed combinations of wage-earners bargaining collectively as to the terms of their employment to be a concomitant of modern industry as normal, inevitable and permanent as power-driven machinery or an urban civilisation. Industrial democracy carried the war into the enemy's camp. Trade Unionism had been denounced, and was to .be denounced again, as an obstacle to economic progress. Trade Unionism, the Webbs retorted, so far from being the enemy of industrial efficiency, was actually its ally. By prescribing minimum standards of employment, which no employer, however hard pressed or unscrupulous, could evade, it diverted competition from exploiting human beings into channels more compatible with social well-being; stimulated technical improvements; and, by levelling up, not only social well-being, but economic efficiency, increased the real income of the nation. Few historical or economic works can expect a life of as much as ten years. The Webbs' books on Trade Unionism contain some statements and interpretations which may need, in the light of later work, much of which they inspired, to be qualified or recast. They remain, however, after the lapse of half a century, not only alive, but incomparably the best English books on the subject. That successive generations of readers should have learned to see the world of Organised Labour through the eyes of authors with the Webbs' profound knowledge of it and faith in its future has been an inestimable service, not only to them, but to the country as a whole.

The bearing on contemporary issues of the great study of Local Government from the Revolution to the Reform Bill seems, at first sight, more remote. In reality, if less obvious, it is hardly less direct. A new chapter in county administration had been opened by the Act of 1888, while the sphere of municipal enterprise was year by year expanding. The Webbs saw in both developments the germs of new forms of collective activity and social provision. It is not surprising that, their work on vocational organisations once completed, they should have turned to explore the history of Local Government. The practical morals for the present which their researches yielded are best stated in the two concluding chapters of *Statutory Authorities for Special Purposes*, with which the students of their ten volumes would be wise to begin. The central theme in their account of the transition from the old order to the new is the transference of authority from little oligarchies of traders and property-owners to representative bodies employing salaried officials to organise the services necessary to health and civilisation for all residents in their areas. It is, in short, the gradual establishment of the citizen-consumer as the dominant power in local government. The conclusion agrees so admirably with the Webbs' own philosophy that the reader is half-tempted to believe that their success in producing at the right moment a lively rabbit from the hat must be due to the fact that they first put it there; but, if they did any conjuring, I, at least, have failed to detect the sleight of hand. It is simpler to believe that history was kind enough to confirm their theories, because from the start they based their theories on history.

They were not of the generals who rarely see the line, and they took their full share of hard fighting, as well as of staff work. Immediate objectives and tactics naturally changed with changing circumstances; and to recount their activities would require a volume, not a lecture. It is sufficient to say that, from the time of their marriage, and, indeed, before it, down to the twenties of the present century, they were never without some campaign on their hands. In the nineties, when the London County Council is struggling on to its feet, one partner not only provides it, in *The London Programme*, with a policy of large-scale municipal Socialism, and himself does more than any other individual to carry it out, but attempts, not without some success, to inoculate the Liberal Party with a virus of Fabianism suitably diluted for infants; writes the Minority

Report which remains the part best worth reading of the twelve portentous volumes of the Labour Commission; and struggles to convert the disorderly welter of London colleges into a People's University. The other, in addition to her work for the same causes, and to the continuous research which was the basis of their practical activities, does what one person can to turn Conservative factory legislation into something not wholly futile. Both, as the principal authorities among economists on Trade Unionism, labour hard to counter the attack on it of which the Taff Vale judgment fired, if not the opening, the loudest, gun, and in the intervals are assisting their child, the London School of Economics, to wrestle successfully with the growing pains of youth.

The early years of the next century were equally strenuous. They saw Webbs' tract on *The Education Muddle and the Way Out*, which helped to supply the ideas for the Education Act of 1902, and the withdrawal next year by the Government of its preposterous first draft of a bill for London, proposing to entrust the service to twenty-eight borough councils, before a storm of opposition in the Conservative Press—a storm which might have astonished ministers less could they have heard the question which Sidney once put to me: "Did you know that for a week I was editor of the *Daily Mail?*" They saw also, what was not less important, the launching of the programme for a national minimum of subsistence and civilisation, which contained the germs of a multitude of subsequent policies, some partially carried out, others still awaiting application. Then came the epic labours of Mrs. Webb on the Poor Law Commission of 1905–1909, when she fought the Local Government Board and its allies to a standstill; the two famous reports on the Break-up of the Poor Law and the Prevention of Destitution; and the three years' campaign by herself and her husband to extort action on them from a Government whose members disliked their proposals in proportion as they understood them. They had made up their minds at an early stage of the first world war that it could be turned into a watershed, not only in international, but in social, history; and the fourth chapter, which opened in 1915, was not the least crowded. Webb's co-operation with Arthur Henderson on the executive of the Labour Party; his joint-authorship with him of the new constitution of the Party adopted at the Conference of 1918; the two pamphlets from his pen, *Labour and Peace* and *Labour and the New Social Order*, the latter a classic which might with advantage be reprinted today; and the magnificent services which he rendered, in the following year, both to the miners and also—if only it had had the wits to realise the fact—to the general public, by his masterly advocacy of nationalisation on the Commission presided over by Lord Sankey, are high landmarks in the development of Socialist policy. Together with the work of Mrs. Webb on the Reconstruction Committee, and on the Committee on Women in Industry, for which she wrote a report that is still not out of date, they stand out from the sterility of those feverish years like oases in a desert.

With the country what it was—and, it may be, still is—to see reforms carried out at the time when they are proposed and in the form in which they are advanced is rarely given to their sponsors, however skilful and pertinacious; but some of the measures launched and championed by the Webbs, if not all that they were meant to be when they left their hands, staggered at last into port. A legal minimum wage in trades once notorious for sweating; the extension of the services of health, education, and pensions on a scale which, inadequate though it is, would thirty years ago have seemed hardly credible; the abolition of the Guardians and the break-up of the Poor Law long after the authorship of the proposal was forgotten; the admission, in principle, of the responsibility of the State for the victims of unemployment; the prevention of mass unemployment itself, long declared to be beyond the wit of man, now blessed by most economists and endorsed in a White Paper; the tardy acquisition by the nation of the most important of minerals, and the nationalisation of a group of key industries—all these and much else had been not only preached by them when there were few to listen, but turned into workable schemes. Before their retirement, they could have pointed, had they been interested in doing so, to that most convincing of compliments which is paid when former opponents claim the credit for measures once denounced by them, and friends dismiss reforms for which formerly they laboured as antiquated trivialities too commonplace to deserve mention.

In reality, there is nothing which would have interested the Webbs less. Two-thirds of their working lives were passed in a world where not only was Capitalism firmly seated in the saddle, with its prestige undimmed and its *moral* unimpaired, but, outside small circles, the bare possibility of a practicable alternative to it was regarded as, at best, an interesting speculation. Like the scientist who commands nature by first obeying her, they accepted that situation, with all the limitations and disillusionments it involved, in order to end it. They played to the score; did first things first; if successful at one point, did not pause to congratulate themselves, but hurried on to the next; if blocked in their course by an obstacle, did not waste time in lamentations, but found some other path which turned it. They never, however, lost sight of their destination, or forgot, amid all their preoccupations with the dusty business of the day, what that destination was. Studiously moderate in speech; regular in their habits, and frugal in their expenditure; a model of domestic felicity; Beatrice with a touch of ascetic austerity, as of the lay-sister of some order; Sidney with the air of scientific detachment—as though, if suitably fee'd, he not only could, but would, argue any case—which is said to have caused one ingenuous mine-owner to be overheard in 1919 saying sadly to another, "I told you we made a mistake in not hiring that man Webb," these demure representatives of the bourgeois virtues belonged, in reality, to the dangerous handful of human beings, perhaps half a dozen in a generation, who live for an idea. They organised their lives as the servants of a cause for which no labour could be too great, and no task too small.

Between the appearance of *Fabian Essays* in 1889 and the twenties of the present century, the Webbs' version of Socialism became, it may fairly be said, the characteristic British version. As such, it was naturally honoured with hard knocks, from more than one quarter. Convinced by experience that, in an industrial civilisation the extension of collective action, so far from impairing the liberty of common men, is the condition of it, they heard with more amusement than annoyance the conventional reproach of an inhuman indifference to individual freedom. Nor, in reality, was their Socialism the unbending skeleton of bloodless formulae, neatly classified and labelled with

exasperating finality, which set successive generations of young
lions sniffing nervously and sometimes growling angrily, as at
an unnutritious dinner of dehydrated truth. The four-fold
way of the years before 1914—regulation, communal services,
the taxation to extinction of unearned incomes, and a wide
variety of different forms of public ownership—continued to
summarise not too inadequately the main heads of their
programme; but its authors, long after they had acquired the
status of an oracle, returning with collective wisdom—"We
think"—unambiguous answers to perplexed inquirers, remained personally humble-minded. They did not cease to
learn, and later statements of their position revealed concessions
both to criticism and to the teaching of events. Under the
influence of the guild Socialists, they came to give a larger
place to the participation in the conduct of nationalised
industries of the representatives of the workers than at one
time they would have admitted. They were quick to grasp
the significance both of the wartime experiments in State-
organisation and of the capitalist ramp which insisted on
their abolition. More surprising, they underwent a rebirth
when they were over seventy. Not being simpletons, they did
not suppose that the achievements of the Russian Revolution
could be replanted, as they stood, in a different soil and
climate; nor were they at ease in the atmosphere created by
what they described as "the disease of conformity." But the
deliberate adjustment of economic means to public ends; the
reliance on science; the glad tidings, in short, of "planned
production for community consumption" with which, for ten
years after their visit, it was the exhilarating practice of Mrs.
Webb to welcome the coming, and speed the parting, guest,
not only appealed to their intellects, but stirred their emotions.
Their admiration for that aspect of Russian life was genuine
and profound.

It is of the nature of political thought that much of its best
work is topical. It achieves immortality, if at all, not by
eschewing the limitations of time and place, but by making
them its platform. It is both inevitable and satisfactory that
some of the problems with which the Webbs dealt should be
now, partly thanks to them, less urgent than they were, and
that on others, which occupy today the forefront of the

stage, they should have thrown out pregnant hints, while leaving it to later hands to elaborate and apply them. As is not uncommon in the case of great people, their premises were more important than the particular conclusions which they themselves derived from them. The fathers of Socialist thought, both British and Continental, had belonged to the pre-democratic era. With some exceptions, they had passed their years of maturity in the two generations between the Revolution of 1830 and the *Commune* of 1871, or, if a later date be preferred, the third English Reform Act. Their philosophies might enshrine truths of permanent significance. Their conceptions of strategy were necessarily the product of the circumstances surrounding them. The Webbs, whose entry on the tasks of adult life began in the early eighties, accepted in broad outline, without slavishly reproducing them, some of their predecessor's criticisms on the economic order, but rejected their political deductions as generalisations made obsolete by the course of events. They saw, not indeed alone, but with unrivalled breadth of comprehension, that the changes of the intervening period had not only strengthened the demand that governments should assume enlarged responsibilities for social welfare, but were adding year by year new wheels to the mechanisms required to discharge them. To repeat old formulae, while ignoring new facts, appeared to them sciolism. Their life-work was the expression of a habit of mind which, while tenacious in its grasp of principles, was realist, experimental and constructive in applying them. It was to show how political democracy, once established, could grow if it pleased, not, indeed, without arduous struggles, but without chaos or catastrophe, into social democracy.

The truth that social processes, in order to be controlled, must first be understood, and that it is the duty of Socialists to be better armed than their opponents, not only with energy and public spirit, but with knowledge, was the Webbs' first legacy to the causes to which they gave their lives. The second, if less obvious, was equally important. It was the temper and attitude of mind, which they brought to the service of them. Trenchancy and good sense; audacity and prudence; the nerve to take risks for great ends and a reasonable adaptability in the choice of means, are not necessarily antithetic. Sad experience suggests, however, that they are not easily run in harness, and that the proud possessors of one set of qualities too often proceed to stultify them by a resolute refusal to combine it with the other. The Webbs thought both types of character and mentality equally indispensable, and themselves united them to an unusual degree. Like most of us, they would have welcomed the discovery of a short cut to the Co-operative Commonwealth; but they knew too much of social history, contemporary affairs and the nature of their fellow-countrymen to suppose that that recurrent illusion has any basis in realities. While not of the kind to shrink from drastic action when circumstances demanded it, they were impatient of the pretence that mere emotional demonstrations are either action or drastic. With all their belief in Trade Unionism, they never succumbed to the overestimate of its possibilities which was visible in some quarters before the first world war, and lingered, a disastrous legacy, for seven years after it. They had come by the middle twenties to the conclusion that, at least in the case of the more important industries, national stoppages had had their day; and they regarded the events of 1926 as a monumental folly—a generous, and, in the case of thousands of unknown men and women, who risked everything for a principle, a heroic folly—but a folly none the less. Holding that reason, given time, would prevail, and that, in some sense, "morality," as Webb used to say, "is in the nature of things," they regarded truculent vapourings, whether from left or right, with a mixture of aversion and contempt, as revealing, in British political conditions, when not the mere vanity of the *poseur*, an unpardonable bankruptcy of character and intelligence. The remark of Cavour, which Sidney sometimes quoted—"Any fool can govern in a state of siege"—expressed an attitude which he shared.

Having made up their minds that Socialism could be made to come in England by the processes of democratic government—of course suitably accelerated—and could not be made to come by any other, they were at pains to exemplify in themselves and to encourage in others the mentality and habits which democracy requires. They made a practice—the first essential—of treating with respect opinions which they did not share. In the distant days when the question of rate-aid for denominational schools caused gnashings of teeth, Sidney, himself an agnostic, lost some valued friends by supporting the principle. His duty, he said, was not to some children, or to most children, but to all children; and no child should suffer, if he could prevent it, from over-crowded classes and insanitary buildings, merely because its parents' convictions differed from his own. As a member, nearly twenty years later, of the Commission on the Coal Industry presided over by Lord Sankey, which met almost daily for five months in a glare of publicity, and on which feelings sometimes ran high, he did not pull his punches; but his refusal to resort to the controversial tricks, by which most of us endeavour to put our adversaries in the wrong, was a model for all who heard him, and the letter which he subsequently received from the leader of the other side, thanking him for his unfailing fairness, was a credit to both of them. In dealing with those of their own not too easy household, both he and Mrs. Webb were consistently unsectarian; insisted that the points on which British Socialists are agreed are both more numerous and more important than those on which they differ; and were tolerant, not only of opponents, but—a more difficult accomplishment—of embarrassing friends, possibly with the reflection that a large dose of imbecility is a necessary ingredient in any movement which aspires to be representative. Themselves formidable in debate, they cared too intensely for the cause to be interested in winning dialectical victories. They took as much pains to make Socialism acceptable to the weaker brethren among their fellow-countrymen as have some of its more voluble exponents to render it repulsive to them.

The Webbs' belief in democracy, however, was a creed not less exacting, but more exacting, than most more truculent evangels. They did not under-estimate the severity of the struggle which lay before the Labour Movement, and cherished no illusions as to the resourcefulness of its opponents. They knew from experience that one of the trades—by no means the least profitable—of which the plutocracy is master is lion-taming by kindness. Not the crudities of forcible repression, but flattery, blandishments and caresses, which would ensure, if the animal succumbed to them, that there would be nothing to repress, seemed to them the gravest danger. It was against these arts of seduction that Mrs. Webb, when a minister's wife, made a characteristic protest, and that her husband, in an article written shortly after he left office, uttered his warning of the perils of "the aristocratic embrace." Independence of spirit, and a contempt for the discreet, gentlemanly bribes employed to undermine it, were, in short, as essential a part of their testament as the belief in knowledge. They have not done the job for us, but they have given us some of the tools, both intellectual and moral, with which to do it.

10

The War and Social Policy[1]

ROM the struggle of Athens with Sparta to the Thirty Years
War, and from the latter to the last great upheaval before
those of the present century, comments on the social
consequences of war have not been lacking. But observers who
recorded the fact of its impact on civilian populations rarely
in the past possessed the materials or techniques, even if they
had the wish, to measure the dimensions of the disturbance
caused by it. We feel, as we read them, the confusion of the
trampled ant-heap; but at the cost to countless lives of the
blow descending on them, and the prophylactics if any, applied
by authority to limit or repair its ravages, we can hardly, in
most cases, do more than guess.

Dr. Titmuss' *Problems of Social Policy*, admirable in its combination of industry with critical power, assembles a mass of
authoritative information which throws a flood of light on these
and kindred topics. Nor is it only the war-time achievements
and failures of British social policy which are illumined by it.
Some of the specifics applied at the height of the crisis lost
their significance when the fever had run its course; but others
have retained it. Hence the book is a study, not merely of
emergency expedients, but of a critical chapter in the growth
of the so-called Welfare State. Sociology, like history, is a
department of knowledge which requires that facts should be
counted and weighed, but which, if it omits to make allowance
for the imponderables, is unlikely to weigh or even count them
right. Dr. Titmuss is a humane scientist, who does not succumb

---

[1] 1950, a review published in the *New Statesman and Nation* of R. H. Titmuss,
Problems of Social Policy (H.M.S.O. and Longmans, 1950).

to the temptation to "measure the Universe by rule and line."
His subtlety and insight in interpreting his evidence are as
impressive as the meticulous scrupulousness with which he has
performed the heavy task of collecting and sifting it.

The second world war was not a bolt from the blue.
Historically, it was the second wave of a convulsion which,
with intervals of comparative quiescence, had been in motion
for the better part of forty years. But it was known that it
would possess some unprecedented features. Long before the
establishment, in April 1935, of the Air Raid Precautions
Department, it was realised that air attacks to disorganise the
life and break the *moral* of large cities would play an important,
and possibly a decisive, part in the enemy's offensive. Apart,
however, from the lessons of the eighteen small raids on London
in 1917–18 and of the Spanish Civil War, evidence by which to
judge the effects of the new technique was not too abundant.
It is not surprising, therefore, that misconceptions should have
existed as to the relative importance of the different consequences of mass bombing. Obviously it would cause both loss
of life and material destruction. The first was overstated. It
was put by the Air Staff as 50–70 casualties per ton dropped,
which produced, as the German air force grew in strength, a
figure in the region of 600,000 killed and 1,200,000 wounded
during sixty days, or over nine times the civilian deaths and
five times the injuries in the whole six years 1939–45. The
multitudinous problems of the social dislocation created by the
second—homeless populations deprived of shelter, warmth, food,
water, clothing and the decencies of existence—were greatly
under-estimated.

A third miscalculation appears to a child of nature more
surprising. The reaction of the lower deck to Nelson's famous
signal that their country expected them to do their duty is
reported, by a doubtless unveracious legend, to have been
expressed in the words: "Does the old bitch think we shan't?"
Needless to say, no phrase so coarse could have soiled the
blameless lips of Ministers; but was it really necessary for a
sub-committee of the Imperial Defence Committee to consider
the prevention of "a disorderly general flight" by the expedient
of throwing a police cordon round London? Where were these
fools brought up, and what did they take us for? It should be

added, in fairness to the politicians, that science was not slow to confirm their fears. The Ministry of Health was informed by the Mental Health Emergency Committee that sufferers from mental and nervous disorders would, in the event of war, "increase to an extent never before experienced." A second group of experts warned it that psychiatric might exceed physical casualties by three to one, which, as Dr. Titmuss drily remarks, would have meant, on the Government's estimates of killed and wounded, "some three to four million cases of acute panic, hysteria, and other neurotic conditions during the first six months of air attack." The medical director of a well-known institution pronounced it "clear to everyone that there must be an immediate inundation with cases of neurosis on the declaration of war, and certainly after the first air raid." Actually, the author observes, "up to the end of 1948, no evidence was forthcoming to suggest any dramatic increase in neurotic illnesses or mental disorders in Britain during the war. The air raids of 1940–41 did not lead to a rise in the number of patients with such illnesses attending hospitals and clinics; in fact, there was a decrease. There was no indication of an increase in insanity; the number of suicides fell; the statistics of drunkenness went down by more than one-half; there was much less disorderly behaviour in the streets and public places." His question, "were not the experts too remote from the ordinary people of Great Britain?" appears, in the light of the facts presented by him, to hit some nails on the head. It is a pity that he cannot hit some heads as well.

The energumen who sets the stage for Dr. Titmuss is, of course, the *Luftwaffe*. The three leading characters in his drama—evacuation, help for the victims of air attacks, and the hospital service—dance to the unmelodious pipings of that presiding demon. The first was not, it seems, the blow in water that is sometimes suggested. It makes all the difference in a tight corner to know that a way out is open, even if one decides not to take it. Like deep shelters to those who preferred to sleep or lie awake at home, evacuation served as a safety-valve. In the author's phrase, it "had the function of shock-absorption." The disparity between the preparations made and the advantage taken by the public of them remains, nevertheless, surprising. Transport and billets for 3,500,000 persons used, in

the first weeks of the war, by less than 1,500,000: the return of
two-thirds of the latter, including nine-tenths of the mothers
with children, in under five months; the small scale, after mass
bombing had begun, of the subsequent migrations—these and
similar paradoxes had not been foreseen. They offer food for
reflection.

Tolstoi somewhere remarks that the much-discussed burning
of Moscow in 1812 needs no explanation. It was merely what
happens of itself when a city is deserted. Somewhat the same
might, perhaps, be said of the fate of the official evacuation
schemes. There were the innumerable individual difficulties,
uncertainties, doubts, fears, disappointments and grievances
inseparable from the up-rooting and re-planting of a population
less numerous, indeed, than anticipated, but not much smaller
than that of New Zealand. There were the effects produced—
in English conditions, inevitably produced—when two con-
trasted cultures were suddenly forced into intimate contact with
each other. To many Parisians evacuation would have meant
no more than returning home. To many Londoners, children
or grandchildren of country people though not a few of them
were, it appeared a sentence of exile. There was the fact that
the authorities, naturally and properly, had thought, in the
first place, in terms of safety, not of welfare. They arranged and
executed, with admirable efficiency, the intricate job of trans-
porting a million and a half children and mothers to regions
out of danger. It was not till later, when the damage had been
done, that adequate attention was devoted to the establishment
in the reception areas of the conditions required in order that
both might live happily in them.

Dr. Titmuss gives their due weight to these and other
influences; but, in speaking of the reluctance to abandon
London and of the tenacity shown under the strains involved in
clinging to it, he lays his heaviest emphasis on a more positive
factor. A rhyme too rude to quote pays tribute to three creatures
who, "the more they're beaten, the better they be." A fourth,
which might be added to them, is the institution of the family.
Like religion, the family is an aspect of life whose deceitful
quiescence in tranquil times cajoles successive generations of
bright intellects into paeans or dirges on its supposed demise,
but which revives, when hit, like a watered flower. If the blows

are sufficiently violent, it displays, to the confusion of the prophets, an almost blood-thirsty vitality. It is here, in the solidarity of the family, that Dr. Titmuss finds one secret both of the early collapse of the first evacuation scheme and of the social cohesion behind resistance. In settled societies, the family has local roots; and few who observed their neighbours in the autumn of 1940 could fail to be struck by the power which such associations supplied. To some of those who knew the other kind of war the humdrum, weaponless routine of London existence, with, as its sole exhilaration, that supplied, after the feeble rejoinders of the first few nights, by the slowly swelling voice of one's own guns behind one, seemed at first the wrong atmosphere to fight in. They were mistaken. In reality, the unbroken contact with familiar things and faces, in an environment charged with a life-time of memories, was a source of inner peace and strength. It preserved intact a thread of spiritual continuity which, but for it, might have snapped. The tranquillity of an aged couple fetched from their blazing house and intent for the next hour on consoling their absurd little dog, who was pardonably dismayed by the racket around him, or the exasperating pertinacity of a pre-possessing, but pig-headed, young woman, who insisted on returning along not too healthy streets on the chance of retrieving her rosary from the rubbish, are two examples out of thousands. Courage is admirable, not because it is rare, but because it is common. It reveals, being common, the true nature of man.

The self-arrested exodus meant the continued exposure to risks of injury from the air of four-fifths of the individuals at first expected to escape them. A second and more important, factor aggravating the difficulties of civilian protection consisted in the unanticipated character of the provision which, as the war unfolded, was found to be required. The Government had expected to meet its gravest problems in the casualty clearing stations. It encountered them in the streets. It had insisted on the hospitals somehow making room for the victims of civilian bombing up to a figure put, in 1939, at 300,000. It discovered that, for every person wounded, several hundred were rendered homeless, and that, while it was dealing with the minor issue by paying for thousands of unoccupied beds, the organisation for grappling with the major one remained to be created under heavy bombing, if not out of chaos, out of not much more than the rudiments of order.

To say that the result was a brief interlude of painful confusion, described by Dr. Titmuss in some moving pages, is not to cast aspersions on the authorities concerned. Every war has its own personality. The distinctive peculiarities of each of the monsters cannot fully be foreseen, but must be learned, like those of an individual, by observing over a period of time the proceedings which reveal them. No reader of Dr. Titmuss's book can fail to be impressed by the wisdom, as well as by the zeal and energy, shown by most of the departments concerned, in particular, perhaps, the Ministry of Health, which, though sadly cramped by antiquated precedents, managed the staff-work of the civilian front. The hero of the air-war—a soldier's battle—was the common people; but their officers, once they had grasped its unfamiliar realities, did not let them down too badly. There are, it is true, some communications from the Treasury which read like the effusions of a senile bachelor descended from a long line of maiden aunts; but, though blankets for the occupants of shelters and sanitary conveniences for children were not, perhaps, the best ground to choose for an exhibition of the gentle art of digging toes in, grandmother, it must be admitted, had something to say for herself. Prudent house-keeping in a war of unknown length, with every service clamouring for preferential treatment and the spectre of inflation round the corner, is no joke. The duration of the ritual teeth-gnashing, which in peace would have continued for decades, was rarely intolerable. Once it had subsided, she seems on most occasions to have come to heel with the dignified composure of a well-educated retriever.

Apart from the tragic background hinted, though not laboured, in Dr. Titmuss's book, the most striking feature revealed in his picture of civilian England at bay is that long ago epitomised in the oft-quoted observation that "war is a rough school-master." A government, when the struggle opens, cannot improvise a philosophy adequate to it. It acts on the assumptions as to social expediency accepted by it in peace, not because they are either edifying in themselves or appropriate to the emergency, but because it possesses nothing else to act on. Then temperatures rise, and the seed beneath the snow begins to sprout. Criticisms ignored in the past are recalled; proposals long cold-shouldered acquire an unexpected relevance. Both bear some fruits. Thus the principles with which a society comes out of the furnace are rarely quite the same as those which it carried into it. Some of the innovations are, of course, discarded, once the ordeal is over. Others remain and grow.

The gradual, unpremeditated, emergence from a morass of obsolescent cant of new conceptions of the social contract is a recurrent theme of Dr. Titmuss's pages. At first, it lingered. Ten years had elapsed since the Poor Law had, in theory, been "broken up." But the sanctity of the principles supposed to be embodied in it had been for a century one of the darling superstitions of the British governing classes. In 1939, those principles still cast their spell. "It was inconceivable," according to this philosophy, writes the author, "that the accident of war, even with the bomber thrown in, would alter the fact that the poor would still be poor and the fortunate still fortunate." Incredible though it seems, the task of arranging provision for the homeless, whose ranks were swollen nightly by the ministrations of the German air force, began by being envisaged primarily as a problem of Poor Relief. It was the Public Assistance Authorities who on September 1, 1939, were first invited to organise "feeding-stations"—elegant phrase—and temporary shelters for homeless people. It was under the Poor Law Act of 1930 that the authorities in question exercised such powers as they possessed to take the action required. It was from staffs engaged in Poor Law work that, at the start of what was to become a group of new services, the *personnel* to run them was largely drawn. The diet supplied in centres was based at first on that of casual wards. "No question of poor relief has so far arisen," brightly reported an official *à propos* of housing damage by enemy planes. The venerable distinction between "natives" and "refugees" from the area of another authority was jealously maintained. Its effect in confounding worse the happily brief confusion can be imagined. The initial limitations on the scope of authorities in the matter of re-housing are almost as astonishing. It had been expected, apparently, that most bombed-out families would find fresh accommodation for themselves, though how they were supposed to set about the job Heaven only knows. Hence, though authorities were given powers to billet, they were at first instructed to use them only in the last resort. In addition, they were informed, in a surprising sentence, that they were not to requisition houses "in advance of the occasion for which the property is required." One bomb, one house?

A society must build with the materials, intellectual and moral, as well as physical, which lie to its hand. These points are mentioned, not in any censorious spirit, which would obviously be out of place, but for a practical reason. They offer a base-line from which to measure the advance of the tide. The process by which, in less than a couple of years, London had created a system of services for the homeless—rest centres; re-settlement; repair of houses; clothes and furniture; mobile canteens, and, not least, trained workers—of whose humanity and efficiency any city might be proud, is recorded at length by Dr. Titmuss. That achievement—not the least of the glories which history should recall—is rendered the more impressive by the level from which the start was made. His chapters on the development of the Hospital service are equally instructive. The features of it first to strike the layman, though to the expert they are, doubtless, platitudes, are two. The first is the pre-war ignorance of essential facts. The kind of war anticipated demanded a pooling of resources in order to meet the abnormal strain to be thrown upon them; and, before 1939, the original idea of a division of functions between base hospitals under the Ministry of Health and casualty clearing stations managed and partly paid for by local authorities had sensibly been discarded in favour of a policy which placed on the Ministry the responsibility for both. But the most effective utilisation of buildings, equipment and personnel required "a marshalling of the assets." It involved the possession by a central authority of full information as to the quantity and quality of the hospital provision. Down to almost the eve of the war, if not, indeed longer, complete information as to the 2,000 odd institutions concerned, was still, it appears, to seek. The second feature emerging from Dr. Titmuss's pages consists of the difficulties arising from the co-existence of what were in effect two separate systems, differing sharply, not only in their histories, but in finance, organisation and outlook, of which one, that represented by the municipal institutions, provided two-thirds of the beds, and the other, the voluntary hospitals, supplied the remainder. Much is said, not without justification, of the inconveniences of the dual system in education. The impression left on a reader of Dr. Titmuss—though he himself says nothing so profane—is that, for good, hearty, stubborn, organised unreason, the hospitals left the Churches standing.

Hospital accommodation was in short supply before the war. The problem, therefore, which confronted the Government, was at once simple and insoluble. It was to meet the normal needs of the sick, while, at the same time, providing for war-injured civilians and wounded soldiers. The authorities did their best. They attempted to secure the 300,000 additional beds which, it was thought, would be required, by clearing patients from some existing hospitals; by crowding beds and adding extra ones; by improving many of the institutions by the supply of additional equipment; and by the erection of new accommodation in the shape of annexes. For the achievements of the Medical Emergency Scheme—a triumph of bold and ingenious organisation—no praise can be too high. But the central enigma remained. In past wars the civilian could make room for the soldier. Now both were at risk, while the sick continued with us. The latter, of whom some 140,000 appear to have been sent home, while new cases—an ever-lengthening list—were denied admission, suffered severely. The voluntary hospitals, which had been disposed to refuse the chronic sick in peace, were even more reluctant to receive them in war. The public hospitals, being under a statutory obligation to accept all patients, could not take the same course. Hence a situation arose in which the former might have empty beds, while the latter were congested. The Ministry of Health, on its side, was unable to grapple with the resulting maldistribution of patients, resources and medical *personnel* by insisting on the extension of civilian work in voluntary hospitals. It could cut down the number of beds for casualties reserved in them; but it was without the legal power to compel their use for ordinary civilian patients. Thus two issues were underlined. The first was the limitation of the powers of the Ministry. The second was the defects of the traditional dualism. The significance of both for the future needs no emphasis. The Health Act of 1946 was to be partly their child.

The care of the homeless and the hospital service were not the only points at which ancient ice began to thaw. By the end of the war, writes Dr. Titmuss, "it was increasingly regarded as a proper function . . . of government to ward off distress and strain . . . among all classes of society. Because the area of responsibility . . . had widened, it was no longer thought sufficient to provide . . . a standard of service hitherto considered appropriate for those in receipt of poor relief—a standard . . . attuned to a philosophy which regarded individual distress as a proof of social incapacity." He cites as illustrations in one sphere the conversion of school meals and milk from a meagre concession to exceptional need into a normal function, the national milk scheme for young children and expectant mothers, and the measures for the provision of vitamins, and allied foods; in another, the higher pensions for the aged, the removal of the latter from the machinery of the poor law, the abolition of the household means test, and the humanising of the spirit of social service administration. "The pooling of national resources and the sharing of risks were not always . . . applied; but they were the guiding principles."

To share risks is easy; but it is not enough. It is necessary also to be eager to share advantages; and the conviction that advantages which are shared are not advantages at all is, in England, deeply ingrained. It has left profound marks on British social policy. Educational organisation is a monument to its power. It cannot be said that the government of Colonial peoples has been—to speak with moderation—untainted by it. Ministering, as it does, to pride and selfish greed, it is a sin the full price of which has not yet been paid. The only cure for it is a recognition that the most important aspect of human beings is not the differences of circumstance, income and race, or even of character and intelligence, by which they are divided, but the common humanity which unites them. The book of Dr. Titmuss on the social consequences of the war is not without some lessons for peace.

I I

Christianity and the
Social Revolution[1]

*C*HRISTIANITY and the Social Revolution is an impressive
book, but it does not lend itself to a brief review. It ranges
in its survey from the origins of Christianity to German
National Socialism. Metaphysics, natural science, social and
religious history, all find a place in its pages. The sixteen
contributors to it include socialists, Christian and other, social
reformers, and communists, as well as philosophers, scientists,
and men of letters. Of its eighteen chapters, some are carefully reasoned essays, others affirmations of their authors'
faith, or faiths. Its unity, therefore, is that of an inquiry
prompted by a common conviction of the importance of the
subject indicated by its title, not of common intellectual
premises or of an agreed body of conclusions.

In that conviction the authors are unquestionably right. The
crisis of Europe today has some resemblance to that of three
centuries ago. Till recently unthinkable, a modern version of the
so-called Wars of Religion is now not an impossibility. The
world, it seems, is dividing itself into credal blocks, of which
some, at least, act on the detestable maxim *cujus regio, ejus
religio*, and destroy freedom to preserve unity. Nothing is
more important than that the nature of these creeds should
be understood, and that they should, if possible, understand
each other. It is the antipathies and affinities of two among

---

[1] November 1935, a review published in the *New Statesman and Nation* of *Christianity and the Social Revolution* (Victor Gollancz & Co., 1935). I have rewritten part
of this review in the light of conclusions reached since it appeared.

them, Christianity and Socialism, which are the subject of this book.

All creeds suffer at the hands of history a double deformation. They undergo a process of dilution and petrifaction—dilution by the world, petrifaction by the elect. On the one hand, their teaching, as it is absorbed into the atmosphere of succeeding ages, loses the sharpness of its outlines and the purity of its colour. Paradoxes, in order to be assimilated, must be turned into platitudes; the coin becomes worn in proportion as it circulates. On the other hand, the more novel their contribution, the more certainly predestined are they to be the victims of their adherents. It is a wise prophet who knows his own gospel by the time that his disciples have shown their devotion by defending it. The faithful in all movements are disposed to believe that they have acquired an exclusive title to expound, not always without glosses, the sacred books, and that fervour of conviction is a sufficient guarantee of infallibility in interpretation. The result is too often that every virtue in the doctrine is preserved except its vitality. Ritual formulae are remembered, and principles forgotten. Reiteration is regarded as a substitute for creative thought. The terror of the orthodox is converted by his followers into the founder of a new orthodoxy.

Christianity has repeatedly succumbed to this degeneration. Socialism, in spite of its short life, has also experienced it. In considering the relations between the two, certain simple canons should be observed, which are as obvious as they are neglected. Facile syntheses are to be distrusted. Each creed may at bottom have more in common with the other than the militant spokesmen of both would wish; but, if so, the affinity must be sought in regions too profound to yield their treasure without a struggle. Each, again, is to be judged by its essential features, not by the *chronique scandaleuse* of failings, crimes, and aberrations which every student of history finds no difficulty in compiling. Religion, or pseudo-religion, can undoubtedly be the opium of the people, as, when Marx and Kingsley so described it, it frequently was. But so also can Marxism, or pseudo-Marxism; few political organisations have been more thoroughly doped by a dogma into solemn and pretentious futility than the party long proclaimed to be the one faithful guardian and interpreter of the inspired Word, the pre-1914 German Social Democrats. Theory, in the third place, must be compared with theory, and practice with practice, not the theory of one system with the practice of another. Finally, no creed or society is to be judged by the absurdities of its camp-followers. It is possible that Christians have talked hitherto more nonsense than Socialists. There are more of them, at least on paper, and they have been longer at it. But in England, at any rate, some Socialists appear to be doing their best to make up for lost time. The eagerness of intellectual snobs to keep in step with the latest fashion on the so-called left is as ridiculous as the frenzies of the nice, lady-like creatures who babble sweetly of violence, without having the remotest idea what violence is like. It would obviously be unfair to make much of either of them.

From inanities of this kind *Christianity and the Social Revolution* is commendably free. It is serious; does not deal in the small change of controversy; and is honest and sincere. It is out of the question to discuss the different contributions in detail. Probably the best for the reader to start on is that of Professor Macmurray on *The Early Development of Marx's Thought.*

Most English readers appear still to begin their Marx either with *Capital* or with *The Communist Manifesto.* The effect is apt to be like that of measles on a man of seventy. The thing is so inappropriate to their condition that it either knocks them out, or leaves them delirious. The right way to study Marx is the way Marx himself studied. It is to follow the line of his intellectual history. He was a writer who, in his later works, took for granted much that had been the atmosphere of his earlier years, and had gone to form his mind. He assumed, of course, Hegel, of whom Professor Macmurray properly makes much. He assumed the legacy of the French Revolution, and of that, perhaps, one should make more. He assumed also, the acceptance of a mass of ethical ideas. To ignore all this, and to start half-way down the stream, is to make certain of misunderstanding him. It leads, in particular, to a grotesque misconception of his theory of history, and, therefore, of politics.

The parody in question takes several forms. The commonest, I suppose, both among opponents and among some of his popularisers, is that which suggests that, by some mysterious

process of squaring intellectual circles, he made a theory of the
processes of history do the work of a political philosophy. That,
presumably, is what is meant when he is denounced as "un-
moral." The conventional mistranslation of *Die Materialistische
Geschichtsauffassung*—"realist," "objective" or "positive" would
all be better renderings—has, no doubt, something to do with
it. In reality, of course, both the suggestion of the critic that
ethics are in some sense degraded if they are shown to have
economic roots, and the illusion of the uninstructed votary that,
in order to dispose of a concept such as personal liberty—not
to mention justice, honesty, and good faith—it is sufficient to
dismiss it as "bourgeois morality," are equally solecisms. They
have their source in the confusion of origins and values which
lies in wait for the unwary, when, in quest of a creed, they turn
to history to help them out. Clio, a mischievous Muse, greets
them with a twinkle in her eye. When the gods send these
simpletons her way, she chastises them, not with stern rebukes,
but with approving simpers, which incite the delighted innocents to plunge, all a-glow with the conviction that their luggage
is the latest thing in science, into the morass prepared for them.
The servile cult of the inevitable; the "realism"—Heaven help
us!—which idolises success and judges policies, not as right,
wrong or a blend of both, nor even as sense and nonsense, but
as "correct" or "incorrect"; the hatred of heretical initiative
which swims against the stream; the contempt for common
men as the cannon-fodder of esoteric strategies beyond their
unsophisticated wits—such are the familiar stages traversed by
the victims before they sink from sight.

   Die Weltgeschichte ist das Weltgericht: the doctrine which
those words have been cited to support—the doctrine that
history is its own justification and that the triumphant fact
is amenable to no higher court—would have horrified their
humanist author. The facility with which not a few *soi-disant*
disciples of Marx succumb to sycophancies similar in principle,
if different in content, to the nationalist sophistries sometimes
sanctioned by Schiller's famous line is surprising. Marx himself, as his scathing denunciations of capitalist vices show,
was as saturated with ethics as a Hebrew prophet. He used
history in order, among other things, to deflate the pseudo-
universalism of time-serving *doctrinaires*, who identified morality

with a respect for property and canonised as the laws of political economy the nasty habits of cotton-spinners. He seems to have shared the prevalent Victorian view of the inevitability of progress, and writes at times as though each succeeding stage in the evolution of society must be, in some sense, an improvement on its predecessors, which it may be, but also, unfortunately, may not. But he was not so naïf as to fall into the vulgar error of supposing that historical statements are either a substitute for judgments of value, or can be directly converted into them. Nor should anyone else. Both demand a grasp of historical facts, but the latter require something more. They involve some conception of the nature and possibilities of man, which supplies a standard of reference by which such facts are appraised, and which, while using historical *data*, does not depend on them alone. To attempt to replace the verdicts based upon it by a theory of social development is to darken counsel. It is as rational as it would be to hold that, because the mating of the sexes is a biological fact, therefore, the institution of marriage possesses no significance beyond it, or to cite the obvious practical necessities dictating, in the rural communities of the past, an organised reduction of diet at the lean season when last year's supplies were running low as proof that the place in the Christian Calendar occupied by Lent can be adequately explained in economic terms alone.

The truth is, of course, that a movement or institution is to be interpreted with reference, not merely or mainly to the causes which contributed to its growth—though they, too, have their light to throw—but to the ends which it serves and to the qualities which the pursuit of those ends quickens into life. Toleration came to its own in England partly—among other reasons—because compulsory conformity, if practicable in a homogeneous agricultural society, was ruinous in a complex commercial one, with a multitude of different interests each clamouring to lead its own religious life. But it was not less a landmark in civilisation, because it was economically advantageous. Some Puritan parliamentarians defended economic interests by appealing to constitutional precedents as to the true tenor of which they were as mistaken as were Puritan armies in their view of the infallibility to be ascribed to the recently published Authorised Version of the Scriptures. But the job done by both was not a small one. The factory slavery denounced by Oastler and Sadler did not cease to be an abomination because mule and power-loom were technically an advance. There is not much difficulty in showing that the sublime abstractions of the Declaration of the Rights of Man derived their practical significance from the prosaic necessities of a particular stage of economic development. But it remains to explain why the wretched recruits bundled into the thin line of regulars at Valmy astonished their generals, and the world, and themselves, by standing still, when the invincible infantry of the Prussians, with the ghost of the great Frederick at their head, began to advance up the hill.

All this is not so irrelevant a digression as might, at first sight, be supposed. The one view of Man which is fatal both to Christianity and to any social revolution worth making is that which regards him, not as a being with a capacity, if he will use it, for autonomy and responsibility, but as a machine or a slave. Given the acceptance of the platitude that the most important fact about human beings is their humanity, there is, at any rate, a sufficient basis of agreement for controversy. It is perpetually denied in practice in capitalist societies, and in Germany the Nazis have turned that denial into a dogma. It is significant, as Dr. Polanyi points out in an instructive essay, that, in the process of eradicating Communism, they have found it necessary to attempt to eradicate Christianity, and, in order to destroy both, to repudiate as a gigantic aberration the last two thousand years of European history, to the greater glory of some obscure tribes of whom little is known, and that little pretty trivial. Granted their premises, their logic is sound. They have been perfectly right in seeing an irreconcilable enemy in a creed which holds that one must obey God rather than Man.

It is true, of course, that, though first principles are important, they do not carry one far. As the contributors who deal, in some interesting chapters, with the history of Christianity have no difficulty in showing, there have at most periods been large anti-capitalist and quasi-communist elements in its teaching. In order to clear the ground for the modern economic system, it was necessary first to bring the Church to heel. In spite, however, of the saints and prophets, it remains true that, if by the ambiguous word "Church" is meant—as usually seems to be the case—its officers, then its record, with certain conspicuous exceptions, has been pretty black. The Anglican Church, in particular, during the greater part of the last three centuries, has been, and still to some extent remains, a class institution, making respectful salaams to property and gentility, and with too little faith in its own creed to call a spade a spade in the vulgar manner of the New Testament. My criticism of the essays of the two writers who touch on that subject at greatest length is not, therefore, that they are too hard on the Christian Church. On the contrary, they let it off a good deal more lightly than would a slave of superstition like myself. It is that they appear to regard human history in general as a more sober, sedate, respectable, less tragic, sublime, disreputable and desperate, affair than it seems to me. There are moments when I am disposed to doubt whether the world is really quite so tidy and well-lit a lecture-room as virtuous intellectuals suppose. But probably that attitude—to use the chaste terminology favoured by the philosophic authors—is mystic, animistic, fictionistic, subjectively idealistic, and solipsistic. So down, presumptuous human reason, down!

The watershed between creeds which this striking book suggests is not the conventional one. Whatever Christians and Communists may say and do, Christianity and popular Communism—though not, it appears, the official variety—are alike in holding the now unfashionable view that principles really matter. Both have their absolutes. As far as principles are concerned, the division of the future will lie, perhaps, less between different forms of political and economic organisation than between different estimates of the value to be put on the muddled soul of Henry Dubb[1]. What the rulers of Germany and

[1] H.D.: the civilian equivalent of the P.B.I. or poor bloody infantry, i.e. the common, courageous, good-hearted, patient, proletarian fool, whose epic is contained in the well-known lines, "We go to work to earn the cash to buy the bread to get the strength to go to work to earn the cash," etc., and who is worth, except to his modest self, nine-tenths of the gentilities, notabilities, intellectual, cultural and ethical eminences put together. I seem to remember an occasion on which a telegram addressed to Henry Dubb, Labour Party Conference, was duly delivered at the correct sea-side resort. The statement that, on the chairman inviting the addressee to claim it, four-fifths of the comrades sprang to their feet, is, however an exaggeration.

Italy think of him we know; and I suspect that those of Japan think much the same. The Christian Church professes to regard him as a little lower than the angels, a child of God, and the heir of eternal life. But it has shown hitherto no unquenchable zeal to ensure that, in this vale of tears, he shall be treated as what, on its own doctrine, he is. The rulers of Russia have kicked out his old masters; fastened a new gang, equally irremovable by action from below, on his much-enduring back ; increased both the output of wealth and his economic well-being, as well as his opportunities of health and education; advertised police collectivism as, not only a convenient device for keeping toilers on their toes, but the last word in proletarian freedom; and floated their up-to-date imperialist business with the good will of a brief, heroic episode so long wound up that official lying disguised as history can with impunity caricature it. The antiquated tag, "the King is dead, long live the King," is not comparable in balm for the powers of this world with its stream-lined successor, "long live the Revolution, now that it and its liquidated leaders are safely buried." The panic of these potentates lest, in the phrase of the polite Japanese, "dangerous thoughts," born of unimpeded intercourse with his fellow-workers in the benighted West, should disturb poor Dubbski's feeble mind with dark suspicions of a sleight of hand would be amusing if it bore less poisonous fruit.

In the interminable case of *Dubb* v. *Superior Persons and Co.*, whether Christians, Capitalists or Communists, I am an unrepentant Dubbite. So I am in the unfortunate position of being unable to applaud my friends for their vices, which—since their shining virtues will look after themselves—is what friends usually desire. *He hath put down the mighty from their seat and hath exalted the humble and meek.* Pondering that and other indiscretions of a neglected classic, I find it impossible to believe, with some Christians, that the love of God, whom one has not seen, is compatible with advantages snatched from the brother whom one sees every day, or that what they describe as spiritual equality, a condition which they neither created nor—happily—can alter, has as its appropriate corollary economic, social and educational, inequalities which, given the will, they can abolish out of hand. The triumphs of capitalism *à l'Américaine* leave me murmuring "Better fifty years of Europe than a cycle of Cathay." Nor does some logical *lacuna* in my brain permit me to share the conviction of the elect that totalitarian magic, *plus* technological gadgets, will suffice to convert such fragments of liberty and equality as Dubb has contrived to pinch from under the indignant noses of his masters into bourgeois superstitions which a well-regulated mind will surrender without a pang. A Christianity which resigns the economic world to the devil appears to me, in short, not Christianity at all; Capitalism a juggernaut sacrificing human ends to the idolatry of material means; and a Socialism which puts Dubb on a chain and prevents him from teaching manners to his exalted governors a Socialism—if such it can be called—which has more than half its battles still before it.

To the critic who complains that I am hard to please, I can only reply by admitting the indictment, and hope for grace to continue to deserve it. Institutions, whatever the emotions surrounding them, are the product of circumstances, as well as of design. Provided that they are willing to live and let live, peoples whose history and environment have caused them to sojourn for a period in the totalitarian *cul-de-sac* should be regarded by their neighbours with sympathy, not aversion or contempt. The fact remains that the prizes, however glittering, won by way of it, are rarely those which they sought. The means destroy the end. The chicken hatched by them, whatever its virtues, is not a Miltonic eagle, "kindling her undazzled eyes at the full midday beam." Too often it is a disciplined, domesticated fowl, whose eyes its prudent keepers are careful to seal and whose wings to clip, with a notice on its cage, "This is a Phoenix: visitors not to look too close." The truth is that a conception of Socialism which views it as involving the nationalisation of everything except political power, on which all else depends, is not, to speak with moderation, according to light. The question is not merely whether the State owns and controls the means of production. It is also who owns and controls the State. It is not certain, though it is probable, that Socialism can in England be achieved by the methods proper to democracy. It is certain that it cannot be achieved by any other; nor, even if it could, should the supreme goods of civil and political liberty, in whose absence no Socialism worthy of the name can breathe, be part of the price. Whether it is in fact attained or not depends, not on the impersonal forces beloved of doctrinaires, but on human minds and wills. It is a matter, in short, partly of the willingness of Socialists to undertake "the intolerable toil of thought," but chiefly of the good sense, pertinacity, nerve and resolution of the loveable, pig-headed, exasperating Dubb.

Since I am not a fatalist, and regard confident predictions from past history as mostly sciolism, I have not yet despaired of Henry. I consider it not impossible that he may one day wake up; make an angry noise like a man, instead of bleating like a sheep; and in England, at any rate, in spite of scales weighted against him, use such rights as he possesses, which he is more sensible than some of his intellectual pastors in thinking worth having, to win economic freedom. Most of the authors of *Christianity and the Social Revolution* would repudiate with contempt a creed so obviously devoid of scientific foundations. A few, possibly, would agree. I leave it to them and their readers.

12

A Note on Christianity
and the Social Order[1]

I

THE first necessity is that Christians should make up their
minds on three elementary points:

(i) Is there such a thing as a distinctively Christian
way of life, for which Christians, in so far as they are true to
their creed, are bound to stand? Or does Christianity fulfil its
function merely by lending a religious sanction to the conventional ethical standards accepted from time to time by
respectable persons?

(ii) If there is such a distinctively Christian way of life, how
far is capitalist civilisation, with its characteristic institutions,
compatible with it? Or how far is Capitalism itself a counter-
religion, which is opposed to Christianity, not merely in detail,
but in principle and essence?

(iii) If such an opposition exists, is it the duty of the Christian
Church to try the institutions and procedure of organised
society by the standards of its Faith, and, in so far as they are
found wanting, to condemn them openly and without reser-
vations? Or does it perform its task by confining itself to the

[1] These notes were written in 1937, as a contribution to the discussions of a
conference which was to consider among other matters, the attitude, if any, that
the Church should adopt on matters of economic and social ethics. I have made
several modifications in the original draft and some additions to it. My debt to
the thought of two great men, the late Bishop Gore and Archbishop Temple, is
both obvious and beyond acknowledgment.

instruction and exhortation of individuals, while maintaining an attitude of indifference towards social institutions?

II

My answer to these questions is as follows:

(i) There is a distinctively Christian way of life. Its character is to be ascertained by examining the Christian tradition as expressed in Christian teaching and practice at its best. This way of life is not, as appears often to be supposed, identical with what is called "goodness"; for there have been, and are, many admirable pagans, and Christianity is a religion for sinners. It rests on a peculiar—and superficially, at any rate, a highly improbable—view of the nature of the universe. It implies the acceptance of a scale of spiritual values which no rationalisation can make appear other than extremely paradoxical.

It is this paradoxical character of the Christian ethic which distinguishes the Christian view of life from that of the world— from that of the world, not only at the latter's bad worst or dull average, but at its brilliant best. Christianity does not merely bear witness against the failures and vices of conventional morality. It repudiates conventional morality's values, objectives and standards of success. It rejects the kingdoms of this world and the glory of them, not only when, as now, the gilt is off the ginger-bread, but also, as before 1914, in the hour of their triumph.

It is for this reason that Christianity has been, at its best, a dynamic and revolutionary force. It is for this reason also that some of those who have seen deepest into the meaning of Christianity, and have sought to reveal that meaning to their fellows, have been held in all ages by good and sincere men to be criminals. Since they challenge not only the vices, but the conventional virtues, of established society, they appear to the rulers of that society to be *hostes humani generis*, whom it is a duty to silence, in order that civilisation may survive.

> *Die wenigen, die was davon erkannt,*
> *Die thöricht g'nug ihr volles Herz nicht wahrten,*
>
> .   .   .   .
>
> *Hat man von je gekreuzigt and verbrannt.*

The good men have been quite right. The civilisation which they think it their duty to preserve is menaced by Christianity.

(ii) Capitalism is an ambiguous term. The most general characteristic of the arrangements designated by it is, I suppose, the direction of economic activity by the owners of capital or their agents for the pecuniary gain of the owners of capital; but the phenomena described by the word are obviously complex. They are at once a body of technical devices, a form of social organisation, a system of ethical assumptions and doctrines, and a type of civilisation resulting from all three. The character of that civilisation is to be judged, not primarily by what is said about it either by its admirers or its critics, but by the institutions which it creates, the relations between human beings which those institutions establish, and the type of character, individual and social, which is fostered by those relations.

Capitalism, thus defined, has a long history behind it. Each of the phases through which it has passed has been marked by distinctive peculiarities, and no general statement can be equally valid for all of them. It has, doubtless, at certain stages in its career, been influenced by the Christian tradition, though, for historical and psychological reasons, by a one-sided version of that tradition. Nor need the reality of its past services be denied. It superseded an earlier social order, many features of which no Christian can approve. It released imprisoned energies which, if often brutal and destructive, have made, nevertheless, genuine contributions to human welfare. It gave scope for the exercise of qualities some of which are rightly valued. In our day, pressure both from above and from below, by the State and by Trade Unionism, has, on a comparison with half a century ago, mitigated its abuses and restricted its power. Nor, of course, is it implied that all the problems with which the economic and social order confronts the Christian today can be traced to one source, or that all such problems are presented to the same degree by all aspects of Capitalism. On the one hand—to quote only one example—there is the whole body of tendencies and interests represented by the words Nationalism and Imperialism. On the other hand, what is of spiritual significance is, not the machine, but the purpose for which it is used. The question, after all, can be stated pretty simply, however complicated the considerations involved in replying to it. It is whether Capitalism, in the forms in which we know it today, fosters relations between human beings, and aids the growth of human characters, of a kind which the Christian would desire to see encouraged.

Different answers, needless to say, are given to that question. For myself, I find it difficult to answer it in the affirmative. "Modern Capitalism," writes the most eminent of contemporary English economists, "is absolutely irreligious, without internal union, without much public spirit, often, though not always, a mere congeries of possessors and pursuers." Lord Keynes' shaft may be too sharply barbed, but it was not ignorance which chose the target. On the whole, whatever may have been true of its past, Capitalism today, except in so far as qualified by influences derived from other sources and long resisted by it, is not so much un-Christian as anti-Christian, and not least anti-Christian when it summons Christianity to its defence. It has, indeed, like its totalitarian rival miscalled Communism, some of the characteristics of a counter-religion. Its emphasis on the supreme importance of material riches; the intensity of its appeal to the acquisitive appetites, and the skill with which it plays on them; its worship of economic power, often with little regard to the ends which power serves or the means which it uses; its idealisation, not merely of particular property rights, but of property in general; its subordination of human beings to the exigencies, or supposed exigencies, of an economic system, as interpreted by other human beings who have a pecuniary interest in interpreting them to their own advantage; its erection of divisions within the human family based on differences, not merely of personal quality and social function, but of income and economic circumstances—these qualities are closely related to the end which Capitalist societies hold to be all-important. In such societies, as the practice of the latter clearly shows, they are commonly regarded not as vices, but as virtues. To the Christian they are vices more ruinous to the soul than most of the conventional forms of immorality.

The complacent assumption that societies which honour these vices are necessarily more Christian than those which, while repudiating Christianity, endeavour to root them out, is repugnant both to common sense and to the Christian tradition. The tree is to be known by its fruits. Societies are not Christian because the majority of their members are baptised, or because, on public occasions, they pay a ceremonial tribute to Christianity. Nor should the criticism of totalitarian régimes be based primarily on the fact that, while tolerating docile and discreetly conducted Churches, they are officially anti-Christian. In their case, also, the important point is the practical effect of such régimes on the spiritual vitality of the personalities moulded by them.

It is of the essence of Christianity that, when conscience and authority collide, it is to God, not to man, that obedience is due. Christians, therefore, however reluctant to engage in political agitation, are bound to demand that political and social systems shall, at least, be such as to permit the fulfilment of that primary obligation, and have repeatedly engaged in struggles against those which conflicted with it. It would be rash to say that no totalitarian régime can satisfy that condition. Totalitarianism, however, is not a modern invention, but a system of which mankind had a long experience before the present century opened. It has been of the essence of such totalitarian régimes as existed in the past, as it is of those which exist today, that the individual is not protected against the executive and its police by courts independent of it; that, since rulers cannot be removed by peaceful methods, opposition to governments cannot easily be distinguished from treason to the State; and that, as a consequence, loyalty to principles repugnant to the former is liable to entail penalties, not only on the individual asserting such principles, but on his family and friends, which few but the most heroic will venture to incur. The resulting subordination to official dictates is ruinous to spiritual integrity. It means that individuals cannot, save at grave risks, speak what they believe to be true or do their duty as they see it. It also means that the Christian Church is unable to fulfil its functions save in an attenuated form. Its members may be permitted to meet for worship; but the Church is a society. It cannot develop a strong corporate life, if its officers and members can think, teach, learn, work, and live only within such limits as the secular authorities may from time to time prescribe.

These statements are, it is submitted, truisms. It is quite

possible both to accept them and, at the same time, to hold that, in their attitude to property, to the exploitation of human beings for purposes of gain, to the care of the young, sick, and aged, and similar economic and social matters, societies which are officially anti-Christian may have some lessons to teach which Christians would do well to ponder. If so, Christians should repent their own sins, and learn what they can from neighbours whose religious and political principles are repugnant to them. Tyranny and economic injustice are both abominations. Christians are not compelled to choose between them. They can and should repudiate both.

(iii) The duty of the Christian Churches is not only to act on the individual conscience. It is also to affirm openly and ceaselessly that men can fulfil the purpose of God only in so far as they follow what has been called above the distinctively Christian way of life. It is to insist that all forms of economic and social organisation which hinder that way of life, whatever their incidental attractions, stand *ipso facto* condemned, and that it is the obligation of Christians to replace them by others which may cause an approach to it to be less impeded by environmental obstructions than it is today.

It is often asserted that Christianity is not concerned with the economic and social order. The reasons most commonly advanced for that statement appear to be two, one primarily economic, one primarily religious. In the first place, the economic order, it is said or implied, is a system of impersonal forces which move by laws of their own, and to which ethical criteria are irrelevant. In the second place, Christianity, it is urged, is a thing of the spirit; to externalise it is to degrade it. It is to succumb to the facile idealism which suggests that evil, instead of being deeply rooted in human nature, is a superficial accident, which can be finally and completely exorcised by a change in social organisation.

Temple somewhere states the true relation between conduct and prayer. It is not, he writes, that conduct is all-important and that prayer aids it. It is that prayer is all-important, and that conduct tests it. The least inadequate manner in which to conceive the relation between Christianity and the social order, is, it may be suggested, somewhat the same. It is obvious that economic activity is conditioned by the objective facts of the natural world. Christian principles will not put coal where there is none, or cause wheat to grow in a swamp, or make labour badly organised and poorly equipped as productive as labour which does not suffer from these disadvantages. To emphasise a point so self-evident is to labour a platitude. These truisms merely mean, however, that man is not omnipotent, but is limited by his environment. The fact remains that, within the limits set by nature, he can choose between several different types of social organisation. He can organise his industry on the basis of slavery, serfdom, wage-labour and by a dozen other methods; and, in fact, he has done so. He can distribute the product of industry in a variety of different ways; he has done that also. He can encourage the exploitation of the weak by the strong, or take steps to prevent it; can harness economic activity to social ends, or permit it to be the sphere of a scramble for money; can show favour to elegant idleness, or do his utmost to discourage it; can maintain social arrangements which perpetuate and sharpen class divisions, or strive ceaselessly to reduce such divisions to negligible dimensions. As a mere matter of history, he has at different times done all, and, in different parts of the world, he is, in different degrees, doing all today. These things are matters, not of any mystical economic necessity, but of human wills and the institutions which human wills create. Whether a society is rich or poor, favoured or prejudiced by its natural environment, it can organise its social system either more justly or less justly. It implies a somewhat singular view both of religion and of practical affairs to suggest that, when the problem of organising it more justly is under consideration, Christianity is to be ruled out as wholly irrelevant.

The second objection is not more valid. Obviously religion is "a thing of the Spirit." But the social order is also a thing of the spirit. The forms of economic organisation which a society establishes, the property rights which it maintains, the relations between its members which it sanctions—these things are partly the result, no doubt, of a judgment on points of practical convenience; but they also reflect its scale of moral preferences. They, and not the phrases which it repeats, reveal its real convictions as to the manner in which mankind should live. These economic and social institutions, in their turn, largely determine the quality of the individual characters to which the appeal of Christianity must be addressed. Character can, no doubt, overcome circumstances, as those who have had few unfavourable circumstances to overcome are not slow to remind us. But it is extravagant to suggest that men are more likely to listen as individuals to a creed which calls them to a life of service and self-sacrifice, if the social environment into which they are born is dominated by a ruthless economic egotism.

The suggestion that a Church which takes such issues seriously must necessarily succumb to a materialistic Utopianism deserves consideration. It is, doubtless, true that all social systems contain elements which are a hindrance to the Christian life, though it ought to be remembered that certain types of system may have more elements than others by which that life is aided. It is doubtless true, again, that men are disposed to expect more from changes in the mechanism of society than such changes can achieve, and that that temper has been reinforced by the material triumphs won in the course of the last century. In Western Europe and the United States man's struggle with nature has been turned from a series of skirmishes into a mass attack, and the economic system from a feeble instrument, perpetually breaking in his hands, into an engine of extraordinary, and increasing, power. The mentality encouraged by that spectacle in England and America is today less complacent than till recently it was; but it remains one in which it is difficult to recognise much affinity with Christianity. In its cruder manifestations, it appears to substitute the ideal of progress for that of righteousness, and to regard an increase in comfort as convincing evidence of divine favour. That mentality was till recently, more characteristic of the admirers of the existing economic system than of its critics. Undoubtedly, however, it is too prevalent in both, and it exists today to a high degree in the totalitarian régimes, which in this respect, as in some others, have perpetuated the worst features of Capitalism. It is right that the Christian Churches should raise their voice against it. It is proper that they should repudiate the assumption that the evil elements in human life can be completely exorcised, either by a mere acceleration of the tempo of economic progress, or by a change in social organisation which would secure that the fruits of economic progress were more widely shared.

That retort is valid as a criticism on the naïf and superficial optimism against which it is directed. When, however, such illusions have been discarded, the central problem still remains. The truth of the doctrines of original sin and of man's need of redemption requires, no doubt, a stronger emphasis than is sometimes given them. But, granted that man's nature is such that evil is a permanent element in his life, that fact is not a reason for condoning the existence of such evils and incitements to evil as it is within his power to remove. Still less is it a reason for violating human fellowship by tolerating the continuance of institutions which inflict on some men, for the profit of others, injuries and disabilities from which the latter are careful, to the point even of over-caution, to protect themselves. Granted, again, that social reconstruction is not a substitute for the Grace of God, it is not self-evident that men prepare themselves best to receive that Grace by deliberately maintaining relations with their fellow-men which they have been expressly warned by Christian thinkers of undisputed authority are both ruinous to their souls and in flagrant contradiction with the teaching of Christ. Indeed, in so far as they wilfully persist in that attitude, can they without temerity ask for Grace? "He who saves his life shall lose it": self-sacrifice has usually, and not unreasonably, been regarded as a central element in the Christian message. Is it not precisely the sphere of economic affairs which offers the most obvious, if also the most difficult, opportunity for the practice of that virtue? And is self-sacrifice the less obligatory on Christians because, under modern conditions, it demands for its exercise, not merely an individual, but a collective, effort?

The view that this world is, of its very nature, a realm of darkness, divided by an impassable gulf from the Kingdom of the Spirit, and that the Christian is concerned with the latter alone, has a long history behind it, and does not lack powerful exponents today. It is a conception, however, which it is somewhat difficult to reconcile either with the facts of experience or with the doctrine of the Incarnation. Men have always desired to serve two masters. Nothing can, at first sight, be more attractive than the attempt to restrict the claims of Christianity to those departments of life in which they may be expected to encounter least resistance. Such treaties of partition have often been essayed. They are, however, unstable, and they have usually been followed by a nemesis unforeseen by those who urged them. If Christians limit their liabilities, the devil does not. They may throw him the world of politics and business to devour at his leisure, in the hope that, while gnawing them, he will leave such minor morsels as private lives alone. He is not, unfortunately, so easily appeased, nor can human affairs be thus departmentalised. As the State and Society are corrupted, the character of the individual is corrupted with them. At best, he purchases a respite for himself by silently repudiating his responsibility for his fellow-men. At worst, he becomes an active ally of the powers of evil. Few men can have lived long in the world, without having seen such tragedies enacted more than once. A man is happy, indeed, if he has not himself played a part in both.

The truth is that the dualism which draws a sharp line between the life of the spirit, which is the sphere of religion, and the external order with which religion has no concern, is quite unrealistic. It is a false antithesis which is based, not on facts, either spiritual or social, but on muddled thinking and bad morals. Obviously, Christianity involves something more than "a mere change of organisation"; but is it equally certain—as appears so often to be supposed—that it necessarily involves something less? And what, after all, is "organisation"? Social organisation rests ultimately on an immense series of decisions taken by human beings as to the manner in which they and their fellows shall live—decisions ranging in quality from mere acquiescence to deliberate acts of will. No historian will question the appalling power of the established fact. But Christians are the last persons who have a right to be fatalists. Irresponsibility, whether casual or calculated, is not one of the Christian virtues. It can hardly be argued that, in making these decisions, the one fact which Christians must be careful to forget is that they are Christians.

Obviously, again, the Churches are not a humanitarian association or a social reform movement. But, granted that their function is to convert the world to Christianity, the fact remains that the conduct of man in society forms a large part of human life, and that to resign it to the forces of self-interest and greed is to de-Christianise both it and the individual souls whose attitude and outlook are necessarily in large measure determined by the nature of their social environment. Obviously, in the third place, it would be wrong for a Church to take its views upon economic and social issues from any particular class or party, as, unfortunately, some Churches appear to a historian to have done so often and so recklessly in the past. It is one thing, however, for a Church to identify itself with a political party; it is quite another for it to state its own conception of the duties and rights of men in society, and to determine its attitude to the policies of all parties by the degree to which they are in agreement with that conception. It is that second course which it is here urged that the Churches should follow. Unless they follow it, to what quarter are men who take Christianity seriously to turn for guidance?

III

These answers to the questions raised at the beginning of this paper are stated summarily. All of them are likely to be rejected by the great majority of Christians. All I am concerned to plead for at the moment is clarity of thought and definiteness of statement. The present hesitations and ambiguities of all but a small minority of the respresentatives of Christian thought in this country are a humiliating exhibition. It is time that they were ended, and a decisive choice made. Do the leaders of the Christian Churches think that Christianity has any distinctive contribution to make to Western civilisation in its present decline? If they do, then, whatever the cost, they should state fearlessly and in unmistakable terms what they conceive that distinctive contribution to be. If they do not think that, then honesty requires that they should state that they do not. Naturally, it is not suggested that they should commit themselves to pronouncements on matters of mere detail. But principles, after all, are intelligible only in so far as their application is indicated. The one course which is indefensible is to reiterate platitudes in general terms, while declining, for reasons of prudence, to indicate the direction in which, in the circumstances of today, the attempt to apply Christian principles to society would cause men to move. Such evasions disgust sincere men, and bring Christianity into contempt.

IV

In the improbable event of Christians agreeing, broadly and in principle, with the views expressed above on the three questions with which this paper opens, what practical conclusions do those views imply? Questions of method and procedure must be left on one side for separate consideration, till questions of principle have first been settled. Supposing, however, that Christian leaders take the view that it is one of their functions to endeavour to persuade men to reconstruct the social and economic order on a basis more nearly in accordance with the principles of the Christian faith, to what features of the present order should they first direct attention, and in what direction should they seek to advance?

All action, and all teaching designed to influence action, involves a decision (a) as to ends, (b) as to means. The first is primarily a matter of spiritual discernment, the second of technical knowledge. The procedure by which the Christian Churches rationalise their evasion of the duty of attempting to christianise the social order commonly consists in suggesting that, while they are clear as to ends, they are precluded from acting on their convictions by uncertainty as to means. I believe the truth to be the opposite.

Obviously, knowledge is of great importance. Obviously, it is desirable that the Christian Churches should take such steps as may be required to ensure that (a) they have at their disposal the services of advisers who are qualified to give expert guidance on the technical aspects of social issues, (b) that their officers have received an education of a kind which will enable them, without themselves being experts, to appreciate and follow such guidance, when it is given. Nevertheless, it remains true, as the credal war now tearing Europe to pieces has revealed to those so innocent as not to have known the fact before, that the differences which matter most are differences as to ends. Given a clear view of ends, such as the Christian Faith claims—and in my judgment rightly claims—to possess, differences as to means remain important on their own plane, but the difficulties which they present are not insuperable.

Christians have no right to demand complete certainty before they act; the world is not so made. Men acquire light on issues which are still dark, not by waiting helplessly for light to be given them, but by acting fearlessly on such light as they already possess. If Christians will take the lead on those matters on which the Christian conscience cannot really be in serious doubt as to the direction in which it should attempt to guide society, they will have enough work on their hands to occupy them for the next half-century. They may reasonably hope that, by doing their duty when that duty is clear, they will prepare themselves to see their way on issues which today are still obscure. As long as they refuse to take the first steps up the hill, they have no right to complain that its summit is in cloud.

V

Let me suggest, merely by way of illustration, and without pretending to do more than touch on one small corner of a vast subject, four examples of certain matters on which Christians should not find it too difficult to take a definite line, provided that they will consent to be denounced by those whose denunciations they should welcome as an honour. I set them out in the order, not of their importance, but of their easiness, on the ground that one had better begin by being faithful in little. Further, I confine myself to those forms of perfidy to the Christian Faith which most strike an English observer, because they are peculiarly characteristic of himself and his fellow-countrymen; writers of other nationalities, which are free from these vices, would doubtless select other topics for emphasis. Finally, I omit the whole immense subject of international economic relations. The issues involved in it are of vital importance, particularly for Christians; but they require treatment at greater length than the space at my disposal permits.

(i) If there is one matter on which all Christians should be agreed, it is the duty of doing their utmost to secure that the conditions of a good life are enjoyed by the whole of the rising generation. It is not open to question that, if that state of things has been established anywhere, it is very far from having been established in England today.

The neglect of the early years of child life; the prevalence among children of ill-health and defective nutrition; the scandalous condition of many school buildings; the grossly deficient staffing of primary schools; the failure to carry out "reorganisation" as originally proposed, so as to secure to all children secondary education of one kind or another lasting for not less than four years; the early curtailment of the school life, and the premature plunge of large numbers of children into wage-earning employment; the still too prevalent exploitation, for purposes of pecuniary gain, of boys and girls between fourteen and eighteen; the social segregation involved in the existence side by side of two separate educational systems, one for the children of the relatively well-to-do, the other for the children of common persons—all this is well known, and, as I write, continues unchecked.[1] The general character of the measures needed to end these evils (except, possibly the last, on which there is a conspiracy of silence) is well known also. The technical difficulties are not, in most cases, formidable. Nor, in the case of the young, ought class prejudices, powerful though even on this matter they are, to be so obstinately set against change as they are when issues of a more narrowly economic kind are under consideration.

"It were better for a man that a mill-stone. . . ." It ought to be possible for civilised people—let alone Christians—to insist that the young, up to, say, eighteen, shall be treated as *au-dessus de la mêlée*, and to refrain from crippling their development by allowing the vulgar irrelevances of class and income to distort it. Is it too much to ask that the spokesmen of the Christian Churches should throw their whole weight on the side of measures designed to ensure that all children and young persons, from birth to eighteen, shall be assured, as far as social action can secure it, equal opportunities—equal in the

---

[1] The principal changes for the better effected since these words were written have been (a) the improvement, as a result of increased earnings, the extension of school meals and milk, and the school medical service, of the nutrition and health of children; (b) the establishment on paper, though hardly yet in fact, by the Act of 1944, of a system of universal secondary education; (c) the raising of the age of compulsory school attendance to 15, to be followed by a further advance to 16, when circumstances allow; (d) the statutory provision for a system of continued part-time education when full-time schooling ends; (e) an improvement in the conditions of juvenile employment. The evils caused by the deficiency of nursery schools; the continued use of primary schools which should long ago have been scrapped; the under-staffing of primary education; the inadequate supply of good secondary modern schools, and the so-called "public school" system, are still with us.

sense explained below—of making the best of the powers of body, mind and character with which they have been endowed? If technical details as to the measures required are needed, they can be supplied; but the gravest obstacles to be overcome are not on that plane. They consist in an objection—disguised, of course, as a solicitude for "economy"—to spending the increased sums required; in a belief that economic inconvenience will be caused if the supply of juvenile labour is diminished; and, most serious of all, in a conviction, no longer so vocal as in the past, but still a power, that the children of wage-earners cannot reasonably expect to be treated with the same consideration as the children of parents with somewhat larger incomes. They are, in short, selfishness, greed, and spiritual blindness. These are not matters with which the Christian Churches can properly regard themselves as having no concern.

(ii) The vice which paralyses the effort to offer a better life to the young is largely that which poisons other parts of our national life. It is the homage paid to the idea of social class, and to the degrading distinctions which the worship of class creates and perpetuates.

Class is a complicated phenomenon. In England it has two main roots. The first consists of the decaying remnants of the social stratification of pre-capitalist society. The second consists of the newer type of economic inequalities created by capitalism. The latter provides the crude and brutal reality. The former invests it with a sentimental and pseudo-historical glamour. The result of both together is that English social organisation and policy, whatever the decorous drapery by which the fact is veiled, have hitherto rested on the assumption that common persons, i.e. about four-fifths of the nation, have not the same right to a good life as a privileged minority.

That attitude is more prevalent and more powerful in England than in most parts of Western Europe. It is noxious to the individual soul, for it is the parent both of insolence —never so insolent as when blandly un-selfconscious—and of servility. It is noxious to society, for it destroys the possibility of a common culture, and makes the struggle of classes a national institution. It ought to be particularly detestable to Christians.

Christians are committed by their creed to a view of man, and of his place in the universe, which makes the tolerance of class advantages and class disabilities—let alone the idealisation of them customary in England—an essay in blasphemy. On that view, man is at once infinitely great and infinitely small. He is a little lower than the angels, the child of God and the heir to eternal life. He is also a fallen creature, helpless without God's aid, and in need of the redemption which God offers those who turn to Him. In modern language he is both an animal and a spirit. He lives in two dimensions. He is, so to say, amphibious.

Such a creed, if sincerely held, leads Christians to a view of society quite different from that taken by good Pagans, unless the latter have been influenced, as many have been, by the Christian tradition.

It means, in the first place, that a man's relations to his fellow-men in this world are part of his relation to God, and that, if the former are opposed to those which the Christian conscience can approve, then the latter necessarily share their corruption. "If a man love not his brother whom he hath seen, how shall he love God, whom he hath not seen?"

It means, in the second place, that the main fact about man is not that he is an animal, but that he is an animal and something more. The Christian tradition does not deny man's animal nature; on the contrary, it emphasises that nature. But it holds that the most important fact about human beings is not the nature which they share with other animals, but their humanity, which, in virtue of the Incarnation, they share with God. Compared with this capital and overwhelming fact, the differences between the races, nationalities, and classes of men, though important on their own plane, are external and trivial. It is this fact, the uniqueness to the Christian of humanity, which gives dignity to men. Any social arrangement which outrages that dignity, any system or policy which treats some men as ends and others merely as means, any institution which obscures the common humanity of men by emphasising external accidents of birth, or wealth, or social position, is *ipso facto* anti-Christian.

The necessary corollary, therefore, of the Christian conception of man is a strong sense of equality. Equality does not mean that all men are equally clever or equally virtuous, any more than that they are equally tall or equally fat. It means that all men, merely because they are men, are of equal value. It does not mean that all, strong and weak, sane and insane, capable and incompetent, should be offered identical provision. It means that equal pains must be taken by society —i.e. their fellow-men—to make for all the provision appropriate to their needs.

Some of those needs are identical, or almost identical, for all members of a given society, and the provision made for them ought also to be identical. Other needs differ widely from individual to individual and from group to group. In that case the forms of provision should be equally diverse. The essential point—the essence of equality—is that such diversities must be based, not on the accidents of class, income, sex, colour or nationality, but on the real requirements of the different members of the human family. All social systems and philosophies which discriminate between men on the basis, not of individual differences, but of mere externals, are antichristian. They assert that economic, social or biological differences between men are more important than the common humanity which they share as children of God.

On this matter—equality so interpreted and the class system which denies it—the Christian Churches have, on the whole, a bad record. Persons are still sometimes encountered who begin by paying a formal tribute to the truth that, on the Christian view, all human beings are "equal before God," and then hasten to qualify the inconvenient obligations which that phrase might suggest by explaining, with melancholy satisfaction, that, if it does not actually sanctify arrangements perpetuating capricious inequalities among men, it is, at least, quite compatible with them. In order to prove that a principle is invalid in this world it is not sufficient to assert that it is valid in another, and such absurdities hardly require examination. Apart, however, from cant of that kind, the attitude of most Christians towards social and economic inequalities, and particularly, perhaps, the attitude till recently common in the Church of England, leaves a good deal to be desired. For a long period, lasting almost into our own day, that Church, in spite of distinguished examples to the contrary, was so closely identified in sympathy and outlook with the upper strata of society as to create the impression that it was a class institution, committed to the defence of the existing social order. There has been, in that respect, a salutary change during the last generation, which it would be unfair not to recognise. But the old, bad tradition dies hard. It would be optimistic to say that even today, a posture of deference to wealth and social position, and of kindly patronage to common men, is universally recognised by Christians to be the negation of Christianity which in fact it is. The statement that "religion is the opiate of the people" is naturally resented. It is difficult to deny, however, that a good many Christians continue to behave as though it were precisely that which they think religion ought to be.

In so far as such a mentality exists, it calls for repentance, and a repentance which shows its sincerity by coming into the open. The Churches should not be content, as in the past, with mere ambulance work for the victims of class privilege, or, as today, with pleading for minor instalments of reform. They should assert that class privilege, and the gross inequalities of wealth on which it rests, are not only a hideously uncivilised business, but an odious outrage on the image of God. While recognising that change must necessarily take time, they should state frankly that the only objective which can satisfy the Christian conscience is the removal of *all* adventitious advantages and disabilities which have their source in social institutions. They should throw their whole weight into the support of measures calculated to lead to that end.

It is both needless and impossible in a short paper to elaborate details. It is sufficient to say that, in this matter, we are not dealing with unknowns, and that, provided that men are willing to subordinate, in a somewhat larger measure, their private interests—or supposed interests—to the common good, long steps towards the removal of the gross economic and educational inequalities which disgrace our life today are unquestionably practicable. Nor is the objection valid that, at periods of economic stress, the removal of these scandals is unimportant or beyond our means. The truth is the opposite. A well-conducted family does not, when in low water, encourage some of its members to grab all they can, while leaving others to go short. On the contrary, it endeavours to ensure that its diminished resources shall be used to the best advantage in the interests of all. A nation, in so far as it is Christian, will observe the same rule. It will act on the principle that, the smaller the income to be divided, the greater the necessity that it be fairly shared. In reality, of course, the most formidable of the lions at present in the path is neither a lack of technical *expertise* nor a deficiency of economic means. It is a deeply rooted dislike of the principle involved. That attitude is, no doubt, less truculent than in the past it was; but its power for evil is unfortunately, not yet exhausted. It is directly opposed to the Christian ethic, with the emphasis which that ethic lays on fellowship, service and self-sacrifice. The temptation to snatch and hoard advantages, instead of sharing them, is natural to man. Social institutions may either strengthen or repress it. The Christian ideal is that expressed by Wordsworth when he wrote of "joy in widest commonalty spread." Christians should work for a social order whose every-day operation gives practical expression to it.

(iii) A third feature of Capitalist civilisation at its present stage can hardly be regarded by the Christian conscience without grave disquiet. It consists in the excessive power wielded, in the absence of public action to control them, by the small handful of a few thousand—or, if that appears an exaggeration, few hundred thousand—persons who are in a position to manipulate the levers of the economic system. This aspect of capitalism often escapes the notice of middle-class observers, who have no direct experience of it. It is, however, an ever-present reality in the lives of large numbers of wage-workers. A small group of financiers in a capital city can largely determine the level of economic activity throughout a whole country. A great industrial firm, ruled by a dozen directors, can take decisions which effect the lives of several thousand families. A group of mine-owners or manufacturers can, by mere obstinacy, prevent changes vital to the welfare of a population out-numbering, with its dependents, that of New Zealand. The reply that the persons concerned are neither less intelligent nor less humane than the majority of their fellow-countrymen is, doubtless, correct; but it misses the point. The crucial question is that, not of the individuals who exercise the power, but of the nature of the power exercised. Inequalities of power cannot be avoided; irresponsible power can. Such power is in principle and essence corrupting. That at present vested in the rulers of a complex and increasingly centralised economic system is of a kind and degree which human beings are not fit to wield. Encouraging dictatorial habits in its possessors, and servility in those submitted to it, it is spiritually injurious to both. Too often it destroys human brotherhood by dividing society into classes which are ends and classes which are means. Here, again, it would be out of place to discuss the steps required. But, here again, the direction in which Christian opinion should desire society to move can hardly be in doubt. The goal to be sought must, at least, include arrangements which, whatever their specific form, make it evident that the common good takes precedence over private interests and ambitions, and that men are fellow-servants.

(iv) The change of outlook and policy suggested in the preceding sections implies, of course, a corresponding change in the views customary among privileged classes everywhere, and often accepted quite uncritically by Christians, on the subject of property. It implies such a change, because economic and social inequalities, irresponsible economic power, and even the neglect of the welfare of the young, are all bound up with that institution.

There are few topics on which more nonsense is talked than that of property. Statements are still sometimes encountered which defend property in general or attack it in general. They appear to rest on the assumption that all forms of property are equally justified or equally without justification. The assumption is fallacious, and the statements are meaningless. The criticisms, in short, to be made on assertions that "property is sacred" or that "property is theft" is not merely that they are untrue, though, of course, they are. It is that, unaccompanied by qualifications, both of them are nonsense.

In reality, property consists of a great diversity of rights, the content of which is perpetually changing. The most fanatical champion of private property would today be indignant if he were thought to be defending that which historically has been among the most important and profitable kinds of property, namely rights owned by certain human beings over the persons of others. Not only, however, slaves and serfs, but rights of justice, public offices, bridges, ferries and roads, and a multitude of other lucrative monopolies, have all in a not distant past been private property. All have been declared to be indispensable to civilisation, and all, or nearly all, are, in Western Europe, no longer private property. The disappearance of these forms of property has not diminished the aggregate value of the personal possessions owned by private persons. On the contrary, by removing what was in effect a species of private taxation, the abolition of these forms of property has greatly increased it.

There is no ground of principle for supposing that—for example—shares in a company or urban ground-rents are more sacred than investments in the purchase of wardships and marriages, or than the right to compel peasants to grind at the lord's mill or bake in the lord's oven. The question for the statesmen is simply one of expediency. The question for the Christian is also one of expediency, but in a higher sense. He has to judge all institutions, and existing forms of property among them, by the degree to which they contribute to the formation of a Christian character.

Tried by that test, many forms of property will, of course, stand. It can hardly be doubted, however, that, under modern conditions of technique and organisation, others have ceased to perform the social function which in the past belonged to them. On the one hand, when, as in 1946–7, one per cent of the population owns 50 per cent of all private property, property may reasonably be said to have become less the national institution which once it was than the badge of a class.[1] On the other hand, the power which it confers under modern conditions, though less than in some past ages, remains impressive. The modern plutocrat may, if his tastes lie that way, be merely parasitic, drawing dividends from mills and collieries which he has never seen, or he may be a man of affairs, whose decisions determine the economic destiny of thousands. In either case, he is one of a minute class, whose economic interests and social outlook too often separate him from

---

[1] The corresponding figures were 55 per cent in 1936–38 and 57 per cent in 1926–28. The effect of the death duties in diminishing inequality would appear to be less than is sometimes supposed.

the mass of mankind almost as completely as if he lived in another planet. Such a condition of things produces the moral and social evils referred to above. One cannot regard men as brothers, unless, in some measure, one shares their lives; and there is good authority for saying that, unless one loves one's fellow-men, it is not possible to love God. Equally serious, the reverence for property of the anti-social type described becomes an idolatry which leaves little room for any more genuine forms of religion. The worship of money, as everyone knows, is inimical both to good manners and to culture. It ought to be recognised that it is equally prejudicial to other sides of spiritual life. The leaders of Christian thought should take the initiative in emphasising the truism that, while some forms of property are to be approved by the Christian conscience, other kinds of property are to be condemned by it. Nor is the cant phrase, which describes property as "a trust," a felicitous defence. A trustee who administered an estate at his own discretion would find himself in gaol, while the property-owner who does so in England may end—if the estate be large enough—in the House of Lords. The important point of principle is to discriminate between property for use and property for power or exploitation, a distinction which largely, though not wholly, coincides with distinctions based on magnitude. The former—the forms of property ordinarily, if inaccurately, covered by the term personal possessions—may reasonably be regarded as, in the conventional phrase, "an extension of personality." To apply the same defence to urban ground-rents or to shares in a great combine is a piece of immoral mysticism.

Christian thought should prick that absurd and repulsive bubble. Some forms of property which today are privately owned—for example the means of production in certain major industries—ought to be publicly owned, because, as long as they are privately owned, the mass of mankind are dependent, to a degree incompatible with human dignity and self-respect, on the will of their owners. Some other forms of property—for example books, furniture, pictures and household possessions— ought to be owned on a much larger scale by a much larger number of persons, because, until they are so owned, the mass of mankind are starved of the necessaries and amenities of a cultured existence. Marginal cases will, as always, present a problem; but a long road—unfortunately—remains to be travelled before that difficulty becomes serious. When we have taken the first, obvious steps towards a more Christian society, we shall be in a better position to decide as to the next.

VI

To state principles without indicating their relevance to specific situations is irresponsible. The illustrations cited in the present memorandum have been included for that reason. The significance of such examples is, however, particular, local and transient. The validity claimed for the Christian doctrine of man, his dependence on God, and the relations which, as a consequence, are to be desired between different members of the human family, is universal and permanent. Capitalism, in its present form, is a brief episode in the history of mankind. Economic appetites, social habits and legal institutions impeding a Christian way of life existed before its rise and will survive its decline.

The world of today will not last. The forces undermining it, forces moral and intellectual even more than economic, are too strong. The methods by which, subject to unforeseen catastrophes, mass unemployment can be prevented; poverty, in its grosser forms, abolished; disparities of health, education, income and circumstances greatly diminished, and services necessary to the general welfare brought under public control, are not a secret. They remain to be elaborated in detail, but in principle they are known. It must be expected that, in a not remote future, a systematic attempt will be made to apply them. The result, in so far as the effort succeeds, will be a society differing sharply, in some significant respects, from that of today. The principles stated in the preceding pages will, in such circumstances, retain their validity, but new interpretations of them will be added to old.

"Give me neither wealth nor poverty, but enough for my sustenance." Experience suggests that, as those oft-quoted words imply, neither an unceasing struggle against destitution, nor a privileged immunity from the trials of the common lot, offers the environment most conducive to spiritual health. A society free from these morbid extremes may legitimately, on that ground, be preferred by Christians to one in which the temptations presented by such contrasts are an ever-present reality. But the effect of conditions depends on the response to them, and the response on the way of life which those experiencing the conditions decide, when a choice is open to them, to choose. It would be naïf or dishonest to pretend that the blots on our national life most commonly denounced by critics of Capitalism are confined to the classes who have hitherto reaped the largest harvest from it. On the contrary, if the target of attack is the economic egotism which snatches private gains at the cost of neighbours or the community, then the mentality which condones such sins, though doubtless more conspicuous in some groups than in others, is widespread.

It is conceivable that a change in social organisation may alter the incidence of the disease without weakening its virulence. A capitalist combine can practise corporate selfishness, but so can a trade union. If a condition of something approaching full employment were established, both the power and the responsibilities of Organised Labour would be greatly increased. It might abuse the former and ignore the latter. Self-indulgence, irregular habits, scamped work, gambling and other futilities, the attempt to take from the common pool without an equivalent contribution to it—such failings are not more edifying in a million wage-earners than when displayed by a handful of monopolists, speculators and urban landlords. Poisons do not cease to be poisons because transferred from the list of luxuries to that of articles in general demand. A redistribution of wealth which merely substituted for a small number of large injections of these toxins a large number of small ones would not in itself be tidings of great joy.

Nor is the formula often hailed as the watchword of a new order free from ambiguity. Equality of opportunity may express either of two distinct ideals, which, when one is pursued to the exclusion of the other, produce opposite results. The opportunities which it is desired to equalise may be opportunities to rise, to get on, to exchange one position for a succession of others, to climb, in the conventional metaphor, the educational or economic ladder. Or they may be opportunities to lead a good life in all senses of the term, whether one "rises" or not. The emphasis of the former interpretation of the phrase is on mobility. Its aim is the establishment of conditions which offer the maximum scope for individual self-advancement. The emphasis of the latter is on solidarity. The society sought by it is one in which, while individuals are free to follow the bent of their talents or tastes, the impulse to seek a new position is not sharpened by exasperation at unnecessary disabilities attaching to that already held, and in which the majority of men are happy to continue in familiar surroundings, because they enjoy in them, not only the economic security, but the dignity, the social contacts, and if they please, the intellectual interests and culture, which human nature demands. The sentiment of the father who hopes—too often, as things are, with reason—that his son will follow any trade but his own illustrates the first view. The attitude of the worker who refuses a foreman's job because it would divide him from his mates is an example of the second. In so far as the Christian life is influenced by external conditions—as, in a world where souls have bodies, it inevitably is—it can hardly be doubted which of these types of social order is least antagonistic to it.

The landscape of the future is necessarily obscure. Since man, as known to history, is a religious animal, the alternative to religion is commonly not irreligion, but a counter-religion. The two great apostacies, the idolatry of riches and the idolatry of power, have had a long reign. If the successor to these pretenders were merely a more widely disseminated cult of betting-coupons, comforts and careers, there might be some gain; but it would hardly be worth the century of sweat which, together with some tears, has been needed to produce it. So dark a future need not at present be foreseen. The noblest aspect of popular movements in this country was expressed by Morris in the passage prefixed to this volume. It has been the unbreakable spirit of comradeship embodied in them. That great tradition makes it legitimate to hope that, when their hour comes, they will produce something better than one more edition of the capitalist farce, which is also a tragedy, of beggar-my-neighbour. But the name of the materialist devil is legion. In the war against him no final victories are won; and, in the more equalitarian society which, in spite of appearances, is already at the door, Christians will not be short of lessons to preach or objectives to attack. In the meantime, they, like other mortals, can best do their duty by playing to the score. They are most likely to win converts to a creed whose kernel is self-sacrifice, if they state its significance for society, not as twenty years hence that society may be, but as it is today.

INDEX